MEMORY QUILTS

DELIGHTFUL WAYS TO CAPTURE TODAY FOREVER

GIFTED STITCHES

One quilt holds the memories of close
friends left behind.

Another marks traditions of our family,
neatly signed.

Efforts best and careful choice were
put into each square.

The life behind a gifted quilt reveals
the joy we share.

A bit of every person gathered once
into a song,

Creates a harmony to which forever
they belong.

The document of patches put together
to display

A past preserved and wonder yet of
days to come our way.

M. D. Robinson '91

POSSIBILITIES

8970 E. HAMPDEN AVE.   DENVER, CO 80231
PHONE: (303) 740-6206   FAX: (303) 220-7424

NANCY SMITH AND LYNDA MILLIGAN

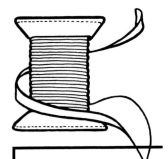

ACKNOWLEDGEMENTS

Supportive Staff of Great American Quilt Factory, Inc.:
Ruth Haggbloom, Jane Dumler, Sharon Holmes, Terri Wiley,
Judy Carpenter, Joanne Malone, Jan Hagan, Peg Spike,
Osie Lebowitz, Aina Martin, Laura Funk, Linda Gutin,
Ashley Smith, Shan Eidsvoog, Kathi Lamkin,
Jan Albee, Judith Wilhelm,
Jean Burkholder

Dedication

We dedicate this book to
the memory of Bruce Austin, a long-time
friend and associate in the needlework industry.
He touched both of our souls with his kind and gentle
nature, his warm humor, his generous spirit, and
his caring approach to life. Our lives were
enriched by knowing him.
We miss him!

Design and Graphics
Marilyn Robinson, Lynn Pike, Sharon Holmes

Photography
Brian Birlauf

Editing
Sharon Holmes

TABLE OF CONTENTS

INTRODUCTION

The making of a MEMORY QUILT or a FRIENDSHIP QUILT is a special way to say *Remember Me* or *Remember When*. These quilts allow us to show in a tangible way our feelings of love or expressions of friendship. These two titles are used interchangeably because the reason for making each quilt is similar. *The Quilters' How-To Dictionary*, written by Marie Shirer and published by Leman Publications, gives these definitions: "Friendship Quilts: group quilts, often made from scraps and varying patterns, that usually have signed blocks. Friendship quilts may commemorate a birthday, wedding anniversary, retirement, or some other special occasion." "Memory Quilts: those which are made to remember people, places, events, or anything else." Our book includes both memory and friendship quilts, and we will refer to them both as MEMORY QUILTS.

Memory quilts have been a part of quilting from the beginning, whether it was a special scrap that was traded between friends; a favorite, worn-out dress that was made into a quilt block; or the signatures of friends on a good-bye quilt. Friends often moved great distances, and communication oftentimes was non-existent. What better way to carry along the memories of friends and family than working them into a quilt, a quilt that when wrapped around a person would envelop her or him with feelings of warmth and support. The scraps of fabric represent the bits and pieces of each memory that was shared, and the stitching of the layers is symbolic of the ties that bind the generations together. Memory quilts became treasured keepsakes to be treated gently and with dignity. As stated in Better Homes and Gardens' *Friendship Quilting*, "A friendship quilt, more than any other, preserves the tradition of fellowship that women have shared over the quilting frame for centuries. The memories and ties sewn into a friendship quilt far exceed its value as a bedcover."

One of the quilted memories that inspired this book is shown on page 35, the first page of a wonderfully inspiring gallery of memory quilts. It is a quilt that Nancy Smith made for the 55th wedding anniversary of her in-laws, Elbert and Roberta Smith. Nancy sent a letter to over 80 of the Smiths' friends and relatives across the country. Along with the letter, she sent a precut 7″ square of white fabric, a few simple directions, and a return envelope. Directions included a few ideas on what the participants might do. Nancy suggested using a memory of the Smiths or a symbol or image that represented a shared experience. Nancy and Jack, her husband, planned to unveil the quilt as part of the anniversary celebration at a family reunion. Seventy-two people returned finished squares. The participants, men *and* women, most of them with absolutely no quilting experience, used a variety of techniques including cross stitch, marking pen, embroidery, photographs, iron-on fabrics, and applique to decorate the squares. The shared memories that came back represented the Smiths' hobbies, including gardening, herbs, golf, and fishing. Favorite vacation spots, careers, nicknames, and colleges were remembered. Each block tells a story. Each block brought back a flood of memories to the participants as well as the recipients. This quilt was truly a scrapbook of laughter, tears, and happy times, a portrait of the lives of two very special people and the friendships they forged on the paths of life. It was, and continues to be, a celebration of friendship.

Because Nancy is co-owner of Great American Quilt Factory, she had the blocks returned to the store. We anxiously awaited the mail as the blocks began to arrive. Along with the blocks came letters and notes recalling memories or simply remarking how pleased they were to have been asked to participate. Jack decided that these notes and letters should be part of the celebration, and he filled a scrapbook that was presented to his parents at the same time as the quilt. Some of our favorite blocks? Jack appliqued nine of his Boy Scout patches to his block. Near the bottom left corner is a block with a sign on it. It represented a sign that the Smiths had once seen. It puzzled us until we read the letter that accompanied the block. The sign said TOTI - EMUL - ESTO. The letter decoded the message as "TO TIE MULES TO". What a delightful memory that must be. Another block, in the middle on the right side, shows an appliqued number one with a hole in it. What else but a *hole in one?*

We can all imagine the flood of memories that this quilt and the accompanying scrapbook brought back to Elbert and Roberta. It was a 55th wedding anniversary shared by highly-valued friends and relatives, and the quilt will become a precious heirloom that will preserve the past for the generations of Smiths to follow.

We were so excited about Nancy's success with this quilt that we started making memory quilts for many different occasions. A very good friend and mentor, Jean Yancey, was having her 75th birthday party which was also to be a benefit for the Encore Organization through the YWCA. We pieced together over 1200 Roman Stripe blocks to be sent with the birthday party invitations. The center strip was muslin, and the invitees were asked to sign their names and send the blocks back to be assembled into a quilt. The quilt would be presented to her at the birthday celebration. Due to postal problems, all of the blocks were not returned on time, so we added unsigned blocks that were autographed at the party. It truly is a living, continuing memory as Jean asks *new* friends to sign squares as well. See the quilt on page 61.

The more memory quilts we made, the more determined we were to write a book, first of all to share the marvelous quilts that we were seeing come through our store, and secondly to help the novice quilter make memories of her own.

Memory quilts can be made for an infinite number of reasons and/or occasions:

 • a baby shower or the birth of a baby
 • a birthday celebration for any age
 • an anniversary of a marriage, business, job, or friendship
 • a wedding shower or wedding gift
 • a healing gift for someone who is ill
 • a remembrance of a loved one
 • a celebration of a holiday
 • a memory of friends left behind when someone moves
 • a special vacation
 • a family reunion
 • a rite of passage (graduation, confirmation, bar mitzvah)
 • a celebration of friendship

This book is meant to be used as a tool to help guide you along the path to making a special memory quilt. It will help you answer the questions: How do I begin? Where do I start? What guidelines should I follow? Who do I want to participate? How long will it take? What size quilt shall I make?

It will be most beneficial if you first read through the book. The sections entitled *The Gallery* and *The Quilts* will help to inspire ideas for your own quilt. The guidelines discussed in the section on organizing will help you avoid possible problems, and the *What Happens If...?* section will help you solve the problems you might encounter. There are sample letters and invitations as well as directions for many different personalization techniques.

Your memory quilt will become the treasured gift of a lifetime. It will convey the spirit of love and the feeling of connection and will make the recipient feel worthy of being honored. The fortunate person who receives your quilt will be able to literally wrap himself or herself up in the affection of the givers. Enjoy the experience of composing the gift of a lifetime!

SELECTING

There are several different types of memory quilts that we show and discuss in this book. Below is an overview of the main categories. Many times a quilt will fall into more than one category, such as a quilt with photo transfers that is also signed. In the section entitled *Personalizing*, the quilts or methods used are described in greater detail. Refer to this section for more information and ideas.

PHOTO TRANSFER QUILTS

There's an exciting element to capturing images on cloth. A quilt made with photo transfers becomes a soft scrapbook or fabric photo album. The many methods of photo transferring allow for endless creativity. A wedding quilt might have a copy of the engagement announcement in one square, the invitation to the wedding in another, and the reception invitation in another. The center block might be a photo of the bride and groom with the surrounding blocks devoted to photos of the wedding party. Another idea could be a baby quilt with a birth announcement surrounded with pictures of the new baby, brothers and sisters, parents and grandparents - a quilted family tree. Add pictures of the family's present home, pets and perhaps some newspaper stories from the "birth" day. What a treasured legacy such a quilt could become for any family! A vacation quilt would be an unusual and distinctive remembrance also. The quilt could include transfers of photos, travel brochures, passport photos, and rail or airline tickets. Souvenirs could be placed in plastic pockets, or photo transfers could be made of them. What fun to explore all of the options!

SIGNATURE QUILTS

A signature quilt is one of the easiest quilts to make and organize for any number of participants. Most people are quite willing to be part of a quilt when it only involves signing their names. Signatures can be added at any step of the quiltmaking process. The *patches* can be signed, the *blocks* can be pieced and then signed, the quilt *top* can be signed, or the *finished quilt* can be signed. The writing space can be small, such as in the "Friends" quilt on page 61, or the space can be quite large which allows for a special saying or remembrance as well as a signature. Throughout the years, signature quilts have been made for a number of reasons. Many were used as fundraisers for an organization. Group or "cause" quilts were used at times to express strong feelings about an issue that was pertinent to the time. Sometimes it was easier for people to make a commitment to an issue by signing their names to a quilt rather than by voicing their opinions aloud. Wedding or dowry quilts have always been popular. To this day they remain a way for friends, relatives and loved ones to express the hope that a bright and happy future lies ahead for the new couple. For a family that was moving, a signature quilt was a way of carrying the love that they felt in their old home to their new surroundings. These kinds of human feelings haven't changed with the passing of years, making the giving of memory quilts as gratifying today as it was in the past. Many signature quilts can be seen in *The Gallery* and *The Quilts* sections.

FRIENDSHIP BLOCK EXCHANGES

Friendship block exchanges are most often done by a group of people who already have a knowledge of quiltmaking. Many guilds have a block-of-the-month program. Whoever wants to participate generally makes a block from a certain pattern using parameters that may or may not be suggested, such as color, background fabric, lights vs. darks, and so on. At the next meeting, a name is drawn, and that person becomes the recipient of the blocks. The Friday Block Party quilting group from Colorado participates in many block exchanges. Pictured on page 36 are several quilts from a Christmas block exchange. They were to make 11 blocks of the same pattern using a muslin background and Christmas reds and greens. They also challenged each other to complete the quilt within one year. Even though the quilts have predominantly the same blocks, they look very different because of border choices and other additions. Some other quilts made in friendship block exchanges appear on pages 41 and 55.

ORIGINAL BLOCK DESIGNS BY PARTICIPANTS

A particularly fun and creative memory quilt comes into being when participants design their own blocks. Sometimes parameters are given to work within, such as size of block and/or background. At other times, the directions may be to "design a block". The participants then use their own creativity to design a block that goes with the occasion or theme. These quilts generally include blocks using all of the personalization techniques that we describe as well as others. A large range in skill level will also be noticeable. "Priscilla's 50th Birthday", pictured on page 50, was made for Priscilla Miller by her friends in the fabric industry. The only parameter was block size, so many techniques have been used as well as many fabrics and colors. The rose sashing and pink borders tie the blocks together. Another particularly beautiful quilt in this category is Barbara Lister's "Arapahoe County Quilters President's Quilt" pictured on page 40. The blocks were made by members of ACQ for Barb, the outgoing president. The parameters in this case were block size and the black solid background. Again, notice the many techniques that were used.

ORIGINAL BLOCK DESIGN OF YOUR OWN

Included in *The Gallery* and *The Quilts* sections of this book are several quilts that were made by an individual or two. In some cases they were made for a special person and in others just for themselves. The memories shared are very personal, such as love for a husband (page 43), or the houses that a family grew up in over the years (page 45). You set your own parameters and choices of memories to portray. You may wish to keep the memories and emotions that surface as you work on the quilt for yourself alone, or you may decide to share them with others. See documentation ideas on page 27.

CHILDREN'S ARTWORK

Any of the types of quilts listed above are adaptable to children, and we have included several memory quilts made in some part by children. In some cases, they have done very little of the work, and in others, they have done the majority of the work. Many of the personalization techniques that we discuss later are very easily done with children, such as stenciling, permanent markers, and fabric crayons. If you wish to make a quilt from your child's artwork, consider hand or machine applique (see "Erin's Quilt" on page 38). Another very easy and successful way of transferring artwork to a quilt is the photo transfer process. Artwork can be enlarged or reduced to make it similar in size, and then it can be transferred to fabric. Other school subjects can be integrated into the construction of a quilt top, making it an ideal learning process. See "Batik Africa" on page 42 and "Reading...The Key to Imagination" on page 79 for more ideas.

ORGANIZING

Below are some questions you need to ask before starting your quilt. As you answer these questions, they may lead to further questions. The answers will help determine the necessary guidelines for having a successful experience. After reading through this section once, return to the beginning and start writing down your answers.

The first question to ask is **For whom do I want to make a memory quilt?** A relative or family member, co-worker or boss, teacher, new baby, high school graduate, community leader, myself? A friend asked us if it was permissible to ask her friends to make a friendship quilt for her. She went on to explain that she wasn't planning on moving, having a baby, remarrying, or anything else that would seem to qualify her to receive such a gift, but she still wanted a friendship quilt. She had been asked quite often to contribute to such quilts being made for others. It made us realize that the only reason you really need to make a memory quilt is to celebrate life, yours or anyone else's.

The second question to ask is **What is the occasion?** The answer may be to celebrate your own life or a friend's life, a birth, wedding, anniversary, graduation or engagement, a special teacher, achievement or holiday. It could also be made as a remembrance for a friend or relative who moves away, or to help you work through the death of someone close to you. The list can go on and on.

When memorable occasions arise, such as significant birthdays or golden wedding anniversaries, people look for a special gift for those who have "everything". By the time people reach seventy-five or are having golden wedding anniversaries, what is there to give them that would be especially meaningful or that they don't already have? On the other hand, one doesn't need to be seventy-five or married for fifty years to deserve such a gift. The quilt pictured on page 77 was made for Nancy's daughter's high school graduation. Rachel had maintained a friendship with two other girls for twelve years. Photos had been taken of the three of them dating back to first grade. Nancy made three quilts using the same pictures in each, one for each girl. The three went away to different parts of the country for college, but each was able to take with her a warm, cuddly memory of their long friendship and good times together.

Who might participate? The only participant may be yourself. The quilt may be made entirely *by* you and *for* you. A "Tea Party at Grandma's", page 48, was made by Sherri Driver to work through her grandma's death. She incorporated fabrics into the quilt that came from clothes her grandma had worn. "Our Homes 1959-1989", page 45, was made by Jean and Earl Scopel to remember all the homes they'd lived in over the years.

When you give a memory quilt to someone, you may want total control; you may want the quilt to come personally from you. The making of such a quilt can be a joy, and you may not want to share it with others. A quilt made with photo transfers for a special person in your life could be a very private walk down memory lane for you personally as you sort the photos and plan and sew the quilt.

Supervising a group memory quilt can provide the person in charge with a very rewarding experience. Participants could be a school class, a scout troup, the people on someone's Christmas card list, business associates, community leaders, sports teams, or neighbors. Again, the list is endless. Please let participants know that perfection is not the name of the game, but participation is what makes it all work. Also, do not make them feel guilty if they do not wish to make a block. It needs to be a pleasurable experience to make a positive memory. Maybe there is another way they can participate. Their special contribution to the memory is what is most important.

Will I have a specific theme? This is not necessary, but if you do have a theme, the participants need to know what it is. The theme may be the reason you are planning the quilt, such as the celebration of a 50th wedding anniversary. The theme may be signatures, a special vacation, homes your family has lived in, favorite flowers, faces of family members, hobbies, history, favorite authors, animals or pets, and so on. Each of the above can then be expanded further to give a more specific focus. The theme of signatures could include signatures of high school friends, names and addresses of a special neighborhood or special written messages. A baby shower theme could be favorite nursery rhymes, lullabies, or special toys. The theme might be hobbies or sports shared with the honoree. Let the participants know the nature of the theme and who to contact if they have any questions. It is helpful for them to know the occasion for which the quilt will be given.

How much time do I allow? It is always a good idea to give yourself a deadline. Many times the deadline will be set for you if you are planning the quilt to coincide with an event such as a wedding or a family reunion. Other times the deadline might be flexible: a baby quilt planned to include photo transfers made from photos of the baby in its first few weeks or months of life. This gift could be given six months after the baby's birth and could even include a transfer made from the birth announcement. Whatever the circumstances, it is definitely a good idea to set a deadline that will give you the motivation and incentive to carry through with the project.

The easiest method we have used for setting deadlines is to start with the date you want the project totally completed. Next, break down the steps for making the quilt: washing fabric, pressing, cutting, piecing, assembling, quilting, and binding. If you are making the entire quilt, you will not have to allow for mailing time and possible kit-assembling time. Work backward from the final deadline and set a deadline for each step. Allow an extra week or two at the end for unexpected circumstances such as illness, unavailability of materials, postal delays, procrastinators (including yourself), as well as participants who might be out of town. If you are working with a group, it will work best if you set one deadline for yourself, but give the group an earlier deadline. Even so, it is not reasonable to think that all participants will be able to meet your time frame.

We have found that a good rule of thumb, if you are sending out blocks to be sewn, autographed, or created, is to allow participants two to three weeks. If only an autograph is needed, go with a two-week deadline. If they need to create a block, the three-week deadline would be more appropriate. If you allow less time, participants might not be able to fit the project into their busy schedules. However, if more time is allowed, participants often feel that they have so much time they tend to put it off and forget about it or don't do it until the last minute anyway. If blocks are being returned by mail, plan another week to ten days to receive them. Some participants will finish the blocks but not get them mailed immediately, and there may also be postal delays. Be sure to allow for these when setting your deadlines.

If you keep a list of participants with addresses and phone numbers, you can follow up your requests. This can be as simple as sending them a postcard or making a quick phone call to see if they have any questions. Be sure to give them your phone number in case they have questions. Also, do not despair if a block is sent after the quilt is assembled. Oftentimes this will happen. We give several ideas on how these blocks can be incorporated in the section *What Happens If...?* Try not to overestimate your own time and abilities. None of us need to put more stress in our lives by setting unrealistic goals.

block may not be understood by some people; if they use that side of the fabric for the right side of the block, and their decoration in any way pulls up the block, the marked seamline could show when the block is sewn into the quilt. Fusing freezer paper to the back of fabric for signature blocks makes it much easier to write on.)

4. Should I include a direction sheet with short descriptions of other techniques like applique using fusible webbing?...include a bibliography of books and magazine articles about various techniques?

Information that will help you make decisions regarding these guideline choices is included in the section entitled *Personalizing*.

If I am having other people participate, what should I send to them? First of all, decide how much control you want to have. If the sewing ability of the other people is not as good as yours, and this will bother you, then you should probably do everything yourself. If, on the other hand, you want others to participate, then you will need to set guidelines or parameters. The more guidelines you set, the more structured the quilt will be, and the uniqueness of each individual block might be diminished. Again, the procedure is determined by your goals. Some of the guidelines to consider:

1. Fabric - Should I make up a kit with fabric included?...suggest a color scheme?....attach swatches of suggested colors?...let them choose fabrics?...include some suggestions on a direction sheet?...give them the background fabric only?

2. Size of block - Should I send them a precut square so all blocks are returned the same size and with the same background fabric?...send a paper pattern?...include precut templates?...let participants make any size block they want, knowing that I can add borders or frames to fit them together? (Sending a precut square definitely helps when it comes time to assemble the quilt, but a block *can* be pulled up by embroidery and some of the other techniques, and this will make the precut block a bit smaller than the others, so leaving extra seam allowance is a good idea.)

3. Signature blocks - Should I send a kit with precut fabric and permanent marking pen?...send precut fabric only with a direction sheet suggesting what type of marker to use?...include on the direction sheet an outline of the signature area marking seam allowances clearly?...make an outline of the signature block on the direction sheet and include instructions for signing names or messages inside?...use a light box to transfer the signatures onto the fabric using a permanent marker of my own preference?...mark the signature area, seam allowance and a center line on freezer paper and press this onto the back of the precut fabric? (Seam allowances marked on the fabric

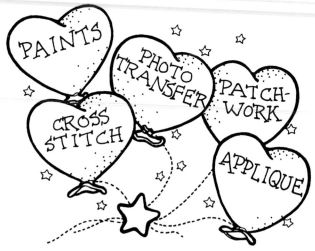

What techniques do I want to use on this quilt? Is this going to be a signature quilt, and if so, what kind of markers will be used? How will you, or can you, ensure that they are permanent? Will children possibly be working on blocks, and if so, can you make it a positive experience for them? If you want the participants to use a specific technique, then you will need to be specific in your directions. Enclose directions, and if possible, illustrations. Be sure to include your phone number so that questions can be answered as they arise. The section entitled *Personalizing* explains many of the most common techniques used on memory quilt blocks. They include:

- signature blocks - embroidered and written
- friendship block exchanges
- patchwork and applique blocks
- photo transfers
- stenciling
- fabric paints and crayons
- fusible applique
- counted cross stitch on evenweave fabric
- counted cross stitch over waste canvas
- special embellishments (badges, buttons, hankies)

Do not be afraid to give the participants choices in their individual blocks. The blocks in "Memories Forever", page 35, the quilt that Nancy made for her in-laws, were made by people seven years old to people in their eighties, both men and women. If people wanted to participate but didn't feel they could, they found someone to help them with their memories. You can make the guideline choices as loose or as structured as you want. The fewer the guidelines you impose, the more creative the quilt may be. There are legitimate reasons for each and every guideline as well as legitimate reasons for leaving out any particular guideline. You need to decide what will work best for you.

What size block will I use, and how large will the quilt be? How many people will be participating? Will there be six participants or 72 participants? If you have six 12″ blocks, there are many ways to enlarge the quilt such as by adding sashing strips, borders, or alternate setting blocks. The only way to make a quilt smaller after the blocks are made is to not use all of the blocks, or the blocks can be made into two quilts. Consider the number of participants, the size of the block you wish to use and how the blocks will be set. All of this must be planned before beginning. For the quilt we made for our friend Jean, we sent to a mailing list of over 1000 people. If they had all chosen to participate, we would have been in big trouble with 6″ blocks. Six-inch blocks set 100 x 100, would have made the quilt 600″ x 600″! We were not out to set a world record. Even with 3″ blocks, we had plans to make a reversible quilt or two quilts. We also considered the skill level and the time invloved and decided that we would piece the blocks ourselves and have the participants just sign them. Many of these people did not even know what a quilt was. Approximately 15 of the blocks were returned with the signatures on the wrong side of the block. Oh well, it made for a funny memory!

What fabrics and colors do I use? Now that you have decided on the theme, the size of the blocks, the techniques to be used, and the size of the project, it is time to consider the fabric choices. The color choices may already be determined by the theme. If so, make sure the participants are very aware of the theme. Unless you want a multicolored scrap quilt, you will have to give the participants some guidelines. You may want to purchase enough fabric to make the participants a kit. This way you are assured that all of the blocks will blend together. Be sure to allow enough for slight mistakes. If you like a scrap look but prefer that the backgrounds of the blocks be the same, make the kit up to include only the background fabric. Swatches of fabric or paints might be sent along as a suggested color palette. When the blocks start coming back, take them to a quilt shop and lay them out on several different fabrics to see which fabric and color will pull the blocks together. Look at the quilts in *The Gallery* for more color ideas.

We have posed many questions that will help you begin to organize a memory quilt. After reading this section, return to the beginning and start writing down your answers. Refer to other sections in this book for more information on types of memory quilts, sample letters, and personalizing techniques. You will find as you go along that some questions will already be answered because of previous choices. If you are not sure of some answers, finish the questions and perhaps some of the unanswered questions will answer themselves.

INVITATIONS

Three suggested formats for inviting participation in your memory quilts are given below. Whichever you choose, be sure to include the following:

- the recipient's name
- the occasion
- the date of the occasion (or the event to celebrate it)
- what you want the participant to do (guidelines, suggestions for embellishment, theme)
- what materials you have enclosed
- instructions for use of the enclosed materials
- date the item is to be returned
- what to do if they cannot return it on time
- your name, address, and phone numbers (home and work)
- if it is a secret or if the honoree knows about it
- incentive for participation (example: photo of finished quilt)
- return envelope with your name and address on it (return date could be repeated on the envelope in the lower left-hand corner)
- a note explaining why the return date is so important (allows time for assembling and quilting the quilt)

SAMPLE INVITATION TO AN EVENT FOR MAKING A MEMORY QUILT

SAMPLE INVITATION FOR PARTICIPATING IN THE MAKING OF A PHOTO TRANSFER MEMORY QUILT

Dear _____ ,
I would like to invite you to share in the making of a memory quilt for _____ . This is going to be a quilt made up of photos that have been transferred onto fabric. I am asking that you send me one to three black-and-white/color photos of you and _____ . These can be recent photos or from as far back as you want. Baby pictures would be great also. I will make copies of the photos and then have them put onto a transfer material. If you will write your name and addresss on the back of each picture, I will see to it that pictures are returned to you. I have also enclosed a strip of paper on which I would like you to sign your name. I will trace your name onto the fabric squares.
This quilt will be presented to _____ on _____ for their/his/her _____ . Could you please send me the pictures and signature by _____ . If there is a problem with this date, please call. I need the time between the dates to assemble the quilt and have it ready for this special occasion, so please don't delay.
I know this will be a wonderful occasion and a lasting gift for _____ . Thanks for being a part of it.

Sincerely yours,

Send photos and signature to:

Name _____
Address _____
_____
Phone _____
Send by _____ , please. Thanks!

SAMPLE INVITATION/LETTER FOR USE WHEN SENDING A KIT TO BE COMPLETED

Dear Friends,

I am in the process of making a memory/friendship quilt for _____ to celebrate _____ . I would like very much for you to join us. I know that _____ would be so pleased to have you participate. Memory quilts are wonderful personal expressions of love and friendship. The emphasis is on the messages of love and not on the perfection of the techniques. Enclosed you will find the following: _____
Instructions are attached. Remember to sign your block. Please return the finished project to me by _____ . I emphasize the importance of this date because I need to have time to assemble the quilt. If you would like to include any notes or cards to celebrate the occasion, feel free to enclose them as we will present them at the same time the quilt is presented.
If you have any questions, please feel free to call. If you would like to participate but are unable to do your own block, please let me know, and I can give you suggestions or perhaps find someone to do your block for you. Enjoy!

Sincerely yours,

Name _____
Address _____
_____
Phone _____
Please return by _____

13

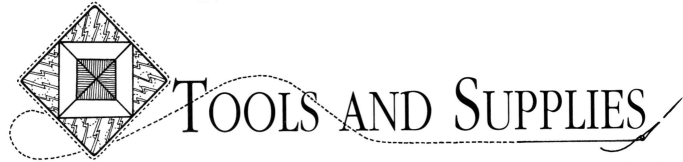
BACKING - the back or bottom layer of the quilt. It is usually 100% cotton dressweight fabric with a medium thread count. Cotton fabric is much easier to hand quilt and seldom allows batting fiber to migrate through the fabric. Sheets generally have too high a thread count, making them extremely difficult to hand quilt. It may be necessary to seam widths of fabric together to accommodate larger quilts. The backing should be 2″ to 3″ larger than the quilt top on each side.

BATTING - a filler used as an interlining between the quilt top and the backing. It provides warmth and thickness. It can be 100% cotton, 100% polyester, or a combination of the two. The higher the cotton content, the more closely the quilt must be quilted. Cotton batting usually has no outside covering on it and thus has a tendency to bunch and shift. Batting is sold in standard bed sizes from crib size to king size or may be purchased by the yard. It is available in white or black. Quality batting should be smooth, even, and of uniform thickness.

BINDING - the fabric that is used to finish the outer raw edges of the quilt.

BLOCK - a complete pattern or design unit. Often a quilt top is composed of many of the same blocks or variations of those blocks sewn together side by side or separated by sashing strips.

BORDER - a separate outside frame completing or enhancing a central element. It is intended to act as the final statement of a quilt. The border can be made of plain, pieced, or appliqued strips. The border can often make or break the total effect of a quilt.

CUTTING MAT - a mat made especially for use with the rotary cutter. It has a self-healing surface and comes in various sizes from 4″ square to approximately 23″ x 35″. Mats are available in various colors, and some are printed with a grid. The most usable size for quilting is a mat that measures at least 23″ wide which accommodates a width of folded, 45″ fabric.

EVEN-FEED FOOT - an attachment for a sewing machine that keeps the top layer of fabric from being pushed ahead of the bottom layer. It is very helpful when machine quilting and when adding binding to a quilt. This attachment is available from sewing machine dealers.

FABRIC FOR QUILTMAKING - The recommended fabric for quiltmaking is 100% cotton. Fabric should be of similar dressweight, closely-woven cottons. These natural fibers age at similar rates, stretch in the same way, and iron well. Cotton is easy to quilt by hand. Fabrics should be prewashed and checked for colorfastness before using.

FABRIC GLUE - an all-purpose glue that works especially well with fabrics. Aleene's™ "Tacky" glue is one example.

FABRIC GLUE STICK - solid adhesive in a stick which is easy to use and works well for many craft projects. Storing the glue stick in the refrigerator will keep it tacky longer.

FIBERS - useful for tying quilts or for adding texture to quilt blocks made for memory quilts. Some types are embroidery floss, perle cotton, fine yarn, and ⅛″ ribbon.

FREEZER PAPER - coated paper which can be ironed to fabric. It is useful for hand applique and for stabilizing fabric before writing on it with permanent marking pens.

FUSING WEB - a paper-backed bonding agent which is released by ironing. Use it to secure fabric to paper, cardboard, wood, plastic, metal, or another fabric. It is especially useful for machine applique. Fusing web is sold by the yard or in prepackaged sizes in craft and fabric stores. Two brand names are Wonder-Under™ and Trans-Web™.

GLUE GUN - an electric gun used to melt sticks of glue which bond surfaces instantly. Guns can be manual or equipped with a finger trigger. Colored glue is also available.

GRAIN - The *straight* grain can either be lengthwise or crosswise. The *lengthwise* grain runs parallel to the selvage. This direction has the least amount of stretch. The *crosswise* grain runs at right angles to the selvage and has some stretch. The *bias* is the diagonal of the fabric, the true bias being at a 45° angle to the straight of the grain. It produces maximum stretch. When sewing with bias and straight grain, put the bias piece next to the feed dog.

INTERFACING - a stabilizer used in fashion sewing and craft projects. Interfacing can be woven or nonwoven, fusible or nonfusible. Most craft projects use nonwoven, fusible interfacing. Nonwoven, fusible interfacing has stretch in the crosswise direction, is stable in the lengthwise direction, and has no grainline. It is sold in various weights for sheer to heavyweight fabrics.

INVISIBLE THREAD - the same as transparent nylon thread or nylon monofilament thread. It is used when an invisible stitch is desired. For machine quilting, use very fine, high quality nylon thread only.

IRON - a tool that is essential for quiltmaking and general sewing. It is helpful to have the soleplate of the iron covered with a non-stick finish. The iron should have a large water reservoir for steam, be comfortable to hold, and not be too heavy.

IRONING BOARD - a surface for ironing. It is preferable to have a well-cushioned board with an adjustable height. The ironing board cover can be plain or printed with a grid. The gridded cover must be straight if it is being used as a pressing guide.

MIRROR MAGIC© 1990 - By using two mirrors set at right angles, it is possible to see what one block reflected into four images looks like. It is equally useful for determining specific miters and multiple star patterns. Directions for a variety of uses are included.

NEEDLEPUNCH/FLEECE - a 100% polyester product used to add dimension to quilted and padded crafts, home decorating projects and garments. It does not stretch like traditional batting and is easy to cut, shape, and handle.

NEEDLES - Hand sewing needles are called sharps and quilting needles are called betweens. Both come in sizes from #5 to #12; the higher the number, the finer the needle. Sewing is easier with finer needles, but they are also harder to thread.

ONE-QUARTER-INCH MASKING TAPE - a special size of masking tape useful to quilters. Use it to temporarily mark quilting lines.

PERMANENT MARKING PENS, CRAYONS, AND DYE STICKS - Permanent markers come in a variety of colors and thicknesses and do not bleed on fabric or fade in the wash. They are excellent to use for signing quilts or making quilt labels. Some markers are specifically for making transfers. Crayons and dye sticks are also available. *Always* test on a scrap first. For more detailed information on some of these products and their use, see page 16.

PHOTO TRANSFER PROCESSES FOR FABRIC - There are several methods for transferring photos to fabric; some involve liquids, gels or a film, and some involve photocopy machines. For detailed descriptions of some of these methods, see page 16. For mail order information, see page 103.

PINEAPPLE RULE - a ruler devised for the construction of pineapple blocks or square-within-a-square patterns. It has horizontal, vertical, and radiating 45° markings which assist in maintaining accuracy in template-free cutting techniques.

QUILT TOP - the front or top layer of the quilt. It can be plain fabric, pieced, appliqued, embroidered, painted, stenciled, or decorated in any way.

QUILTING HOOP - similar to an embroidery hoop but thicker. It is a double wooden circle with a self-contained clamp. The size of the hoop depends on the comfort preference of the individual and the size of the project.

QUILTING STENCILS OR TEMPLATES - used to draw the quilting pattern directly onto the quilt top. Templates or stencils are generally basic outlines or shapes which are filled in with additional detail lines. The shapes can be realistic or geometric and can be used singly or repeated.

ROTARY CUTTER - a rolling, disk-shaped blade that cuts easily through fabric. The cutters come with large or small blades; both work equally well. It is possible to cut up to eight layers of fabric at one time.

SASHING STRIPS/LATTICE/SETTING SQUARES - strips and squares of fabric that separate pieced or appliqued blocks. Setting squares may be placed at corners where blocks come together.

SCISSORS - Sharp scissors are an essential tool for any kind of sewing. Scissors range in size from 4″ to 10″ and are made for right-handed and left-handed use. Fabric scissors should be used only for fabric. Cutting paper, plastic and batting with fabric scissors will dull them quickly. Scissors that begin to bind when cutting fabric will not produce even edges. Layer fabric and cut only as many layers as the scissors will cut accurately and smoothly.

SEAM RIPPER - A ripper with a very sharp blade is preferable as it slices the sewing threads cleanly.

SEE-THROUGH OR TRANSPARENT RULER - the perfect companion tool for a rotary cutter. Rulers vary in length from 6″ to 24″, are usually ⅛″ thick, and are available in numerous geometric shapes. One very useful ruler has ⅛″ marks and is approximately 6″ wide by 22″ long. Angle markings of 30°, 45°, and 90° are also very helpful.

"STITCH-N-TEAR"® - a rip-away backing for stitchery such as applique or embroidery. It prevents stitches from puckering and slipping. Pellon® "Stitch-N-Tear"® is 22″ wide.

STUFFING/FIBERFILL - loose polyester fibers used for filler in various kinds of stuffed work.

TEMPLATE - a reusable pattern piece that serves as a gauge or guide and is usually made from see-through or opaque plastic.

THREAD - For sewing machine work, a strong polyester or cotton-covered polyester thread works best. It is usually easiest to sew with a neutral color throughout, light with lights, dark with darks. For quilting thread, choose from cotton, cotton-covered polyester, and polyester. All seem to work fine, so it is usually a matter of preference. Variety threads like rayon and metallic threads are useful for embroidery, applique, and machine quilting.

USING PERMANENT MARKING PENS, CRAYONS, AND DYE STICKS

For best results when using any permanent marker, follow the instructions printed on the package or on the marketing display. Most of the manufacturers advise the same basic directions listed below. None of the brands imply a warranty, and the buyer is encouraged to do her own testing. The buyer is advised to: use light or pastel-colored fabric washed in warm water with gentle action and no bleach (to remove sizing which if not washed out may resist the ink or cause the ink to bleed); protect the work surface or the fabric underneath with paper; set colors by ironing with hot, dry heat (cover surface with paper or a clean cotton cloth); wash finished test sample in the same way the finished project will be washed; store markers horizontally.

We performed a series of nine separate tests on the brands marked with an asterisk in the list below so that we could be comfortable in recommending them. This in no way means that other listed products would not hold up to the same tests, only that these were the pens available to us at the time of testing. We advise you to perform your own tests using your own fabric and methods. See page 18 for our test information.

*NIJI® FabriColor Superfine Markers - 24 colors; permanent on fabric after 24 hours; prewash fabric and set colors by ironing.

NIJI® FabriColor Calligraphy Tip - 12 colors; 2 sizes (3.5 mm and 5.0 mm); permanent on fabric after 24 hours; prewash fabric and set colors by ironing.

*SAKURA Fashion Craft™ Permanent Markers - brush-style nib for both broad and fine strokes; 24 colors; machine washable; fade-resistant; non-toxic; colors mix; color dries instantly, set by ironing using a presscloth for 2 minutes; recommend prewashed fabric with a minimum of 20% cotton.

*SAKURA IDenti-pen - black, red, gold, and silver; fine and extra-fine points; color is usually opaque.

*SAKURA Micron Pigma 01 Pens - 6 point sizes and 7 colors; waterproof; smear-proof; fade-proof; quick-drying pigment ink. Pigma ink offers the advantages of permanency and true color reproduction. Color should not feather or bleed through the thinnest of fabrics or papers.

*SULKY® Iron-on Transfer Pen - 8 colors. These are transfer pens with the difference being that you draw your design first onto paper and then transfer it to the fabric (if you are using words or numbers, plan accordingly or they will be reversed). Trace or draw any design onto plain paper; iron design onto fabric with a hot, dry iron for 30 seconds using firm and even pressure. Multiple copies can be made from a single transfer.

CRAYOLA® Fabric Crayons - 8 colors. Draw design onto plain paper (if you are using letters or numbers, plan accordingly or they will be reversed); transfer to fabric using cotton setting on iron and a steady pressure. Synthetic or synthetic blend fabrics work best.

PENTEL® FabricFun Pastel Dye Sticks - 15 colors; permanent; washable; avoid 100% synthetic fabrics; prewash. Draw design onto fabric; cover with paper and press with hot iron to set dyes. If a mistake is made, color can be washed out before heat setting.

USING PHOTO TRANSFER PROCESSES FOR FABRIC

We experimented with several different processes for transferring photos to fabric. Each one, when directions were followed explicitly, gave satisfactory results. The method that we preferred was the color laser photocopy method using a material called Paropy™. It gave the most consistent results, and the quality and color of the photos were excellent. As with most things, the technology is changing daily, so we will keep experimenting with the new products that come out.

For best results when using any of the products below, follow the instructions printed on the package or on the marketing display. Most of them use the same basic directions listed below. None of the products imply a warranty, and the buyer is encouraged to do her own testing. Photocopies of photos are preferred over photos themselves for making the transfers, although some methods will work with the actual photos (the process may destroy the photo). These processes work best on light or pastel fabrics. The buyer is advised to prewash the fabric or item inside out with cool water on a gentle cycle and hang to dry; do not dry-clean.

PICTURE THIS™ by Plaid - permanent; washable after 72 hours; works with black and white or color photos. Medium is brushed onto photocopy and placed coated side down on fabric to dry for 24 hours. Paper backing is then peeled off. Another method allows photos to be applied face up thereby eliminating reverse images.

TRANSFER-IT™ by Aleene - Medium is brushed on photocopy and placed face down on fabric. It is dried for 24 hours, heat set for 30 seconds with a dry iron, and then soaked in water so the paper backing can be rubbed off.

BY JUPITER® - A coat of gel is applied to a photo or photocopy. Coated picture is placed face down on light-colored fabric, and pressure is applied with a brayer. When thoroughly dry, fabric is soaked, and paper backing is rubbed off. A thin coat of gel is applied to seal the image. Words and images are reversed. Hand wash only.

TRANSFER MAGIC™ by EZ International - Transfer Magic™ film is applied to photocopy; photocopy is soaked, and paper backing is rubbed off. Transfer is positioned on fabric and ironed with a hot iron. Protective covering is removed, and fabric is allowed to cool for 20 minutes. Largest photo possible is 5″ x 7″.

COLOR LASER COPIER TRANSFERS - We have only worked with a Canon Color Laser Copier and have had remarkable results. Basically, the process is to make a black-and-white or color photocopy of a photo (magazine picture, child's artwork, etc.) on a specially coated transfer paper. Depending on the type of transfer paper used, the image is now ready to be transferred directly to fabric or to another prepared sheet which is then ready to transfer to fabric. We have tested two types of transfer material. Magic Touch™ transfer is a single sheet of transfer paper coated with a polymer emulsion which actually goes through the copy machine. After the photo is copied to this paper, the transfer is placed face down on fabric which has been placed in a heat press. This process needs high heat, 375°, and pressure. We have not successfully transferred Magic Touch™ transfers with a home iron. The other transfer sheet we have used is called Paropy™, and it involves a three-step process. The photo is transferred by the color copier to the "A" sheet. Using the heat press, the image on the "A" sheet is transferred to the "B" sheet. The image on the "B" sheet can then be transferred to the fabric with a heat press or a home iron. Either seems successful with Paropy™, although the heat press works more consistently.

PERSONALIZING

Listed on the following pages are several different techniques for personalizing a memory quilt. These include permanent markers, photo transfers, stenciling, embroidery stitches, and cross stitching, as well as other techniques. Information on piecing and applique will be found in the *Quiltmaking Techniques* section. Because the use of permanent markers and the making of photo transfers involve relatively new techniques, we have expanded on them more than the other techniques. Listed in our bibliography are several books if more information is needed on a subject. We do encourage you to perform your own tests on the fabric of your choice. Also, realize that it is the sharing of the memory and not necessarily the quality of the work that is most important in a memory quilt.

WRITING ON FABRIC

For best results when using any permanent markers or crayons, follow the instructions printed on the package or on the marketing display. None of the brands imply a warranty, and the buyer is encouraged to test using the fabric that will be used in the proposed project.

We performed a series of nine separate tests on the five markers noted with an asterisk in the *Tools and Supplies* section. We tried all of the available colors of each. We used 100% cotton muslin. We performed tests on the following:

- prewashed fabric with signatures (airdried)
- unwashed fabric with signatures (airdried)
- prewashed fabric ironed onto freezer paper and signed
- unwashed fabric ironed onto freezer paper and signed
- heatset signatures (iron set directly on fabric)
- heatset signatures (presscloth dampened with a solution of ½ vinegar and ½ water)

All of the above samples were ultimately washed in warm water with a phosphate-free detergent, rinsed in cool water, and put in a regular clothes dryer. One set of samples was also dry-cleaned. The reason for the freezer paper test is that freezer paper works well as a stabilizer for writing and drawing on fabric. We wanted to make sure that the paper did not change the absorption of the ink into the fabric.

Except for the dry-cleaned sample, the colors remained permanent and were very clear. The Sulky® Iron-on Transfer pens bled a little, but we were using them as markers directly on the fabric and not ironed onto paper first as the directions specify. Some of the lighter, more yellowish colors and the neon colors were harder to read and did not show up as well after washing. The dry-cleaned sample results were less than satisfactory with many colors completely disappearing. The Sakura Pigma pens, when dry-cleaned, kept their color the best except for the red. The majority of the Sakura markers dry-cleaned well, but a few faded or changed color slightly. Our dry-cleaner stated that the colors would fade with each successive cleaning. In view of this, we would definitely recommend that you not have your quilt dry-cleaned, and make sure you give the recipient a care card with your recommendations for cleaning.

SIGNATURE EMBELLISHMENTS

There are several ways to write on fabric to ensure successful results:

1. Tape the fabric to a table or hard surface. It is preferable to use masking tape or drafting tape. Be sure to protect the surface underneath with paper to prevent the ink from marking it.

2. Iron the fabric onto freezer paper. Freezer paper is found in the canning section of your grocery store. It has a shiny side and a dull side. Iron the shiny side onto the wrong side of the fabric. The paper will stabilize the fabric, making it easier to write or draw. Guidelines, such as the size of the quilt block, the seamlines, the center of the block, or even a signature line, can also be drawn right onto the freezer paper. The markings will be very visible through the fabric but will be removed when the freezer paper is peeled off.

3. A rough draft of a drawing or a signature can be drawn on premarked paper. The paper should be marked with the size of the patch or square. Seam allowances should also be marked. The participants can then autograph or draw their pictures onto the paper. Tape the fabric over the paper and trace the design. This method works very well when you want to ensure that a permanent marker is used, because you will be doing the actual marking. It also gives you as many second chances as you need to draw or write exactly what you want without wasting the fabric. This is an excellent idea for children. Because it is much easier to draw on paper, the child can compose his or her picture first and then trace it onto fabric.

Signature quilts can be organized in numerous ways. Often, the more guidelines you can give to the participants, the more successful the project will be. An instruction sheet should go along with the invitation. It should include information on guidelines that you have chosen for the project. Do you want only signatures, or will there be space for messages also? What type of pen will you suggest using? It definitely should be a permanent marker, and perhaps you can give suggestions of brands and where to find them. If participants aren't sure if a marker is permanent or can't find one to use, what can they do? Send an extra scrap of fabric for them to try the marker before writing on the fabric. Advise them to rinse the sample in water to check for permanency. The instruction sheet should also have a drawing of the patch with the seam allowances marked and the reason for not writing in the seam allowance. If you would prefer to use the same marker and don't want to include one with every invitation, have the participant autograph the marked square on the paper and return the paper. When the messages are returned, simply slide the written paper under the fabric and trace the signature with the permanent pen. If necessary, you can use a light box or tape the paper to a sunny window. Another very successful method is to send precut patches with freezer paper ironed to the wrong side. (These patches do not need to be squares or rectangles but can be other shapes such as hearts or hands. See *Inspiration*, page 31.) The freezer paper should have the center of the block, the seamlines, and a signature line marked on it. The paper will help stabilize the fabric for writing, and the placement of the signatures should be consistent.

Another method for signature blocks uses Iron-on Transfer Pens by Sulky®. Do the drawing or signatures on plain paper and then iron them onto the fabric. Because they are transfer pens, everything will be reversed. If you are using them for words, write out what you want to say with a pen or pencil. Flip the paper over and copy the writing, with the transfer pen, so that the writing appears backward. When you iron it onto the fabric, it will be facing the right way. People, including children, often feel more confident if they can draw on regular paper first, because they know they can experiment before actually transferring their design onto fabric.

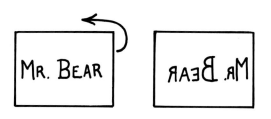

EMBROIDERY

Signatures can be embroidered rather than signed, or a quilt might have a combination of both. Give the participants guidelines as to how many strands of floss to use (usually two or three) and which stitches are best to use. Another option is a professional monogrammer. Monogrammers are listed in the yellow pages of the telephone book. This is an excellent way for people to participate without actually doing the work themselves. Monogrammers can do initials or names, and often they can copy a simple emblem or design or even a saying or poem. Don't forget to suggest this alternative.

We have illustrated several embroidery stitches and embroidery designs that we feel work successfully with signatures. We have also illustrated names on page 18 with several different embellishments. These can be used for either written or embroidered signatures. Please feel free to make copies of these different signature styles to send out to your participants.

EMBROIDERY STITCHES

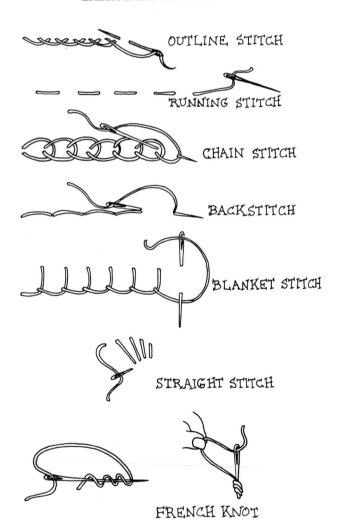

OUTLINE STITCH

RUNNING STITCH

CHAIN STITCH

BACKSTITCH

BLANKET STITCH

STRAIGHT STITCH

FRENCH KNOT

LAZY DAISY

SNOWFLAKE

FOR FUN!

STAR FLOWER

DRAWING AND COLORING ON QUILTS

Be sure to read the information above about writing on fabric. Much of the information applies to drawing and coloring as well. Coloring can be done with fabric markers, fabric crayons, fabric paints, pastel dye sticks, or transfer pens. We discuss some of the brands we tried in the *Tools and Supplies* section. Again, there are many more on the market. Just be sure to follow the package directions and do your own testing.

Fabric markers are probably the easiest to use unless they have an extra fine point. The Sakura Pigma pens are terrific for signing quilts and fine detail work, but you would not want to use them for coloring in a large area. The basic directions are to use prewashed fabric in a light or pastel color; protect the work surface underneath; set the colors by ironing with hot, dry heat and a presscloth; wash in warm water on a gentle cycle; and hang to dry. We tested several different markers for colorfastness. See the results on page 18. The use of markers with calligraphy tips allows you to decorate your quilt blocks with names, poems, special sayings, or personal messages. The special calligraphy tip is designed to make all handwriting and printing decorative and attractive. The markers should be held at a 45° angle. Form the letters without changing the angle of the pen. As with all markers, the ink flow is controlled by working faster or slower.

Fabric crayons are an ideal medium for children as well as adults. The basic directions are to use fabric that is 100%

synthetic or a synthetic blend (100% cottons will work, but the color will not be as bright). For the purest colors, use white fabric or a very clear pastel. Draw the design on a non-glossy drawing paper and color with fabric crayons. For bright colors, use heavy pressure. Shading can be done with the side of the crayon. Rub colors together on the paper to blend and shade before transferring. Place the fabric right side up on top of an ironing pad and lay the paper design face down on top of the fabric. Using a dry iron set on cotton, iron with a steady pressure over the entire surface until the image becomes slightly visible through the paper. Remove the paper carefully. If desired, the design can be reused by coloring over it again. To wash the blocks, machine wash using warm water. Do not bleach or machine dry.

Another product that is fun to use is Fabricfun-Pastel Dye Sticks by Pentel®, available in art supply stores. These sticks can be used directly on fabrics. Avoid 100% synthetic fabric. Apply the dye-stick to the fabric with even strokes in one direction to assure a smooth, unbroken layer of color. Shadings can be produced by rubbing and blending the colors together with your fingertip. Once the design is complete, cover it with a sheet of paper and iron with a hot iron to set the dyes. Color can be washed out before heat setting if you change your mind or make a mistake. After ironing, the design is permanent and washable. You can also use dye-sticks for stenciling. Do not dry in a clothes dryer.

Transfer pens can also be used for drawing pictures. One very good brand is Sulky® Iron-on Transfer Pens. To use, draw and color the design on plain paper with the transfer pens. If words or numbers are part of the design, they will need to be written backward, so plan accordingly. Flip the drawing face down onto the fabric. Iron the design onto the fabric with a hot, dry iron for 30 seconds using firm and even pressure. Multiple copies can be made from a single transfer.

We have included several quilts in *The Gallery* as well as *The Quilts* section that have been made using the above techniques. The quilt entitled "Flower Study", page 48, was done by first graders using fabric crayons. Their teacher, Mary Christofferson, shared with us, "Children were each given a drapery or wallpaper sample with a flower theme. Most of the flowers were not realistic but were more 'fantasy' flowers. Each student drew a flower (with pencil) on a piece of paper, adding stems, leaves and flower details. Next the children were given fabric crayons and told to use several colors, pressing hard." If the children wanted to put their names on the pictures, they put their names or initials on the back of the paper and then went to the window and traced them to the right side. Mary and each student then ironed the picture onto the fabric. It was the first ironing experience for most of the children. In order for the children to get a second print, they recolored all of the parts and then ironed a second copy. As you can see from the quilt, it

was a wonderful project with the children doing most of the design work.

Fabric crayons can be very versatile. The creative techniques that follow have been published by Binney and Smith, Inc., manufacturers of Crayola® Fabric Crayons.

Textural Rubbings - add pattern to areas of design. Lay a piece of paper over any textured surface such as plastic, lace, corrugated paper, screening, or tile floors. Color over the paper with the crayon. Lay the colored paper face down onto the fabric and iron as stated above.

Leaf Prints - reproduce the exact texture of a leaf by coloring a sheet of paper solidly with Crayola® Fabric Crayons. Place the leaf (iron first to flatten) vein side up on paper with the colored sheet on top. Press. The color is transferred to the leaf. The leaf can then be printed onto the fabric. You can also use weeds or other flat shapes found in nature.

Collage - color several pieces of paper with Crayola® Fabric Crayons. Cut out shapes and paste onto a piece of paper. Add lines for detail. The entire design can then be ironed all at once.

Stencil - cut a stencil of the desired shape out of plain paper. Lay the stencil on top of the fabric. Place a sheet that has been solidly colored with Crayola® Fabric Crayons on top of the stencil. Iron over all. The color goes through the cut-out area producing a very sharp image.

STENCILING A DESIGN

Suggested stenciling supplies include acrylic or fabric paint, palette, stiff-bristled brushes, mylar or stencil paper, freezer paper, and a permanent marking pen.

To make a stencil, decide on a particular design. For suggestions, see the two stenciled quilts on pages 39 and 53, made by Kathy Emmel's fourth grade classes, and see the stenciled sashing strips of the quilt on page 46, made by Graland Country Day School. The design can be very simple: a heart, a star, or a geometric shape (see end of pattern section for some examples).

Begin by drawing the outline of the *finished* block on a piece of paper. Draw the design centered in that block. Take a piece of heavy-duty mylar (available in most quilting, craft, or art supply stores) and place it over the paper design. Trace the design onto the mylar using a permanent marking pen; include a line for the outer, raw edge of the block. Put a piece of plain white paper down on the work surface, place a piece of glass over the white paper, and put the mylar with the traced design on top. Use a small mat knife with a very sharp blade. Holding the knife like a pencil, cut the design out following the drawn lines on the paper below. You now have a piece of mylar that is the size of the quilt block. Line up the edges of the mylar with the edges of the fabric block. The design will then be lined up exactly the same on each block.

An alternate method for making a stencil is to use freezer paper. Draw the stencil design exactly as above on white paper. Be sure the lines are dark. Place a piece of freezer paper, shiny side down, over the design (use a piece of paper large enough to include a line for the outer, raw edge of the block). Tape the freezer paper in place. Trace the pattern with a pencil, using a ruler for the straight lines. Cut out the design from the feezer paper using a sharp mat knife. Press the freezer paper stencil onto the block (background fabric) with a dry iron on a medium setting. Press well, making sure the edges are tightly sealed. Proceed with the stenciling directions below.

The above method would work well for defining the design area on blocks that you would like to send partially prepared to participants. (The purpose would be to control the design area, not to stencil the blocks.) The freezer paper stencil would be ironed onto the fabric squares, then the blocks would be mailed. You would peel off the paper when the blocks came back to you. Be sure to include instructions for decorating; participants could fill their shapes with writing, drawings, embroidery, or some other form of embellishment.

To stencil the design, use acrylic or fabric paint. Make sure that the paint is washable and permanent. Again, make your own test to be sure the medium performs the way you expect it to perform. To begin stenciling, squeeze a small amount of paint onto a palette (saucer, aluminum pie tin, piece of wax paper). Using a medium- to stiff-bristled brush, dip the tip of the bristles into the paint. Dab most of the paint off on a paper towel so the brush is fairly dry. Lay the stencil on the fabric and tape it into place. There is also a stencil adhesive available that can be sprayed on the stencil so it sticks in place on the fabric. Using light stroking motions, start painting at the edges of the cut-out area and brush toward the center. It is much better to use several light applications as more can be applied. Shading can be done with thin layers of different colors of paint. Always be sure to brush toward the center, away from the cut edge of the stencil to keep the sharpest painted edge.

The fish stencil used on the quilt on page 39 was stenciled in a similar fashion, but because all the fish were stenciled onto a center medallion area, the students did not need the line for the raw edge of the block. Be sure to allow enough plastic around the cut-out so that you don't paint over the ouside edge. Stenciling is an especially good technique to use when working with children. The sashing strips of the quilt on page 46 were stenciled with the actual design used in the colored blocks. The animal outlines were reduced to a size that fit in the strips, and the children stenciled them.

COUNTED CROSS STITCH

Many of the quilts featured in *The Gallery* have counted cross stitch blocks in them. Many people are already familiar with the technique, and if not, it is very easy to learn. Counted cross stitch as it applies to memory quilts can be done in two ways.

The first method is to cross stitch over waste canvas. Waste canvas is similar to needlepoint canvas. It has an even grid for placing stitches, but after the stitching is finished, the block is placed in water, and the threads are pulled out, leaving the cross stitch design in place on the background fabric. Waste canvas comes in several counts (mesh sizes) and usually has some different colored threads to help with the counting. To use waste canvas, first tape the edges, then lay the canvas on top of the background fabric. Baste into place. Cross stitch the design over the canvas threads. Remove the basting threads and tape. Wet the block and pull out the canvas threads. Allow the block to dry and then press if needed.

The second method is to use an evenweave fabric for the background of the block. If you are asked to make a block for a memory quilt and are not supplied with or told what fabric to use, then you may choose whatever you would like for the background of the block. After deciding on the fabric, measure and mark the cut size of the block including seam allowances. Remember that the seam allowance is ¼", so keep stitches approximately ½" away from all edges. It would probably be best to mark the outside edge of the fabric but not cut it. Evenweave fabrics ravel easily, and enough seam allowance must be left for the person who is to assemble the quilt. The edge can be taped or zig-zagged on the sewing machine to control the raveling. Mark the center of the block with basting threads and complete the cross stitch design.

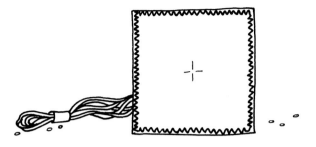

A simple illustration of cross stitch follows. Consult the numerous books and magazines for extra help as well as a local quilt, needlepoint, or cross stitch shop. Basically, counted cross stitch involves two trips across the fabric for every row of completed stitching. Make a row of diagonal stitches beginning at the lower left of each row and ending at the upper right. To complete the stitch, simply go back over the row, crossing the previous stitch and working the diagonal lines from lower right to upper left as illustrated. Other stitches can also be combined with cross stitch such as backstitch and French knots.

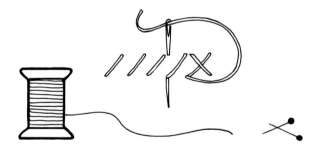

PHOTO TRANSFERS

There are many products on the market that make transfers from photocopies. We experimented with several of them. Refer to *Tools and Supplies* for more information. Experiment with your own method and try the new products that are coming onto the market. Whichever product you choose to use, the method will open up a whole new area for quiltmaking and for creating wonderful memory quilts. As the saying goes, "A picture is worth a thousand words."

We have experimented with two basic types of transfer mediums. One is a liquid that is painted on the photocopy, and the other uses a photocopy printed on a special type of paper. Because a photocopy is made of the photograph, the original is not destroyed. With the more sophisticated copy machines on the market, the design can be enlarged or reduced, the image can be reversed, or a certain portion of the photo can be copied. The clearer the photocopy, the clearer the transfer will be. Drawings and other types of flat material that can be photocopied can also be used to make transfers. Also, the better the color copier, and the more knowledgeable the operator, the better the transfer. Because color copiers operate with a four-color process, each of these colors (magenta, cyan, yellow, and black) can be adjusted to produce the most acceptable color copy.

Photo Transfers Using the Liquid Mediums - Please carefully read the directions for the product you purchase, and follow the steps exactly for the best results. Products with liquids are basically used as follows. The fabric should be pre-washed. Make a photocopy of the photograph (or other material). It can be black-and-white or color. Paint the liquid mixture on the photocopy (in some cases also on the fabric), covering the desired area. Smooth down evenly. Allow the fabric and photo to dry. To hurry the process, use a hair dryer. When all is dry, soak the fabric in a pan of warm water. Rub carefully from the center out, taking all the paper off and leaving the image imprinted on the fabric. Use fingertips, a sponge, or a soft toothbrush to do the rubbing. Continue this process until all the paper is removed. If working with a particularly stubborn spot, add a little baking soda or vinegar to the water to make the paper peel more easily. Do not dry-clean the finished piece. We also found that painting on a diluted solution of the medium helped to seal the final picture and give it a glossier appearance.

Photo Transfers Using The Laser Copier Method - We have found the laser copier photo transfers to be the clearest and the most consistent of all the transfers we tried. The laser copies offer a high resolution image. It is more expensive than other procedures, but it is also the quickest and the easiest. The laser copier method uses a special transfer paper that is coated with a polymer emulsion which can be heat-fused to fabric. To begin the process, a photocopy of the photograph or other material is made on the transfer paper. Then, depending on the type of transfer paper used, other steps are followed.

We have experimented with two types of transfer paper. One consists of a single sheet of transfer paper. The image is transferred to the paper, and the picture is then transferred to the fabric using a heat press (available at T-shirt shops). This method does not work successfully with a home iron. It needs the combination of high heat (350°-375°) and pressure that only the heat press can provide. Photos will be reversed unless the copier being used has a reverse-image feature.

The second type of transfer paper consists of two sheets of paper, an "A" sheet and a "B" sheet. The photo is first transferred to the "A" sheet. The photo on the "A" sheet is then transferred to the "B" sheet using a heat press. The "B" sheet is then ready to transfer onto the fabric. For best results, use a heat press (350° - 375° for approximately 10 seconds) to transfer the image to the fabric. We have also had very good results using a home iron with very hot, dry heat. Experiment a little to see how long it must be pressed. The image is totally absorbed by the fabric and becomes an integral part of the fabric that lasts through washing, drying, and ironing without fading or cracking. Because the design is transferred in reverse to the "B" sheet, the finished picture will be in the same direction as the original, not in reverse, when transferred from the "B" sheet to the fabric. When cool, press using a silicone sheet; this will help to set and soften the design. The silicone sheet may be used up to 12 times. Also use the silicone sheet any time the block needs pressing. For best results, wash in warm, soapy water and hang to dry; press, if needed, using the silicone sheet. Do not dry-clean.

If you cannot find this color copy service or an operator who is familiar with fabric photo transfers, see page 103 for mail order service.

FUSIBLE WEBBINGS

The fusible webbings now in the marketplace have opened up fabric crafting to people without sewing machines and to those who do not know how to sew. Applique blocks can be made in a matter of minutes simply by cutting out the desired shape and ironing it to a background block. The applique, properly applied, won't lift or pucker, and the edges do not need to be sewn or sealed. First, choose the shape that you wish to use. Shapes can come from logos, coloring books, hand-drawn artwork, china patterns, letters of the alphabet, and so on. Trace the pattern onto the smooth, paper side of the fusing web. Trace patterns the reverse of the direction wanted. Press (hot, dry iron) the web to the wrong side of the desired fabric with rough side facing fabric. Cut out the shapes. Peel off paper; position applique onto the background fabric and press again; the applique fuses to the background. If the design is layered, arrange all appliques before fusing.

Experiment with different types of fabric such as felt, lamé, denim, or suede. Read manufacturer's directions before using. Most products can be washed. Again, perform your own tests.

FABRIC PAINTS

There are many fabric paints on the market such as Tulip® and Polymark®. Use fabric paints to personalize blocks, to apply rhinestones and beads, for fabric stenciling, and to seal the edges of fused appliques. The paints are very easy to use, although we suggest practicing a little until the desired width of line is established. The paints are permanent, non-toxic, dry-cleanable, and washable. There is a wonderful range of colors and textures, including glitters, iridescents, metallics, and flourescents. Children, especially, will enjoy working with fabric paints.

SPECIAL EMBELLISHMENTS

Make no-sew appliques from insignias, patches, laces, doilies, or handkerchiefs. Applying these basically flat items to the background block can be simply done with fusible webbings. Lay the item face down on a scrap of brown paper (grocery bag). Cut a piece of fusible webbing slightly larger than the item to be fused. Place the rough side of the webbing against the wrong side of the patch. Press for about three seconds with a hot, dry iron. Excess webbing will adhere to the brown paper. Let cool; peel off paper backing. Position item on the background fabric with the webbing side down. Cover with a damp presscloth and press for about ten seconds.

Trinkets, buttons, sequins, costume jewelry, rhinestones, and beads can also be used for embellishments. These three-dimensional objects can be attached to the background block by stitching or gluing with an electric glue gun.

These techniques are not by any means the only methods of personalizing memory quilts. As can be seen from the photos in the gallery, you are only limited by your imagination.

QUILTMAKING TECHNIQUES

FABRIC PREPARATION

Fabrics of 100% cotton are highly recommended for quilting. All washable fabrics should be laundered before being used in a quilt. Determine if fabrics are colorfast by handwashing separately in detergent and warm water. If the water remains clear, fabrics may be washed together. If any fabric bleeds, wash it separately. If fabric continues to bleed, discard and select another fabric. After checking for colorfastness, wash fabrics in a washing machine with warm water and a mild detergent; rinse well. Since most shrinkage occurs in the dryer, tumble until nearly dry. Press using steam and spray sizing if necessary.

PRESSING

In quilting, seams are pressed to one side or the other. The standard ¼″ seam allowance used in quiltmaking makes it difficult, if not impossible, to press seams open. In addition, the quilt is more durable if seams are not pressed open. It is preferable to press seams toward the darker fabric. If this is not possible, make sure dark fabric seams do not show through the quilt top by trimming a scant amount off the dark seam allowance.

1. Press patchwork on the back first using steam and a gentle, up-and-down motion. Swinging the iron back and forth tends to distort and stretch patchwork. Then turn block or quilt top over and press gently on the right side.
2. When pressing block seams (seams joining one block to another), press all seams in the same direction for one whole row. On the next row, press all block seams in the other direction. This will allow seams to fall in opposite directions when machine sewing one row to another row.
3. When ironing row seams, press the entire seam length of the row in the same direction, always being careful not to stretch the fabric.
4. When ironing border seams, press all seams toward outside edges. A final pressing of the quilt top will make it easier to mark the quilting design and will make potential problem areas visible.

CUTTING FOR MACHINE PIECING
Template Method

1. Make templates using typing paper or graph paper to include ¼″ seam allowances.
2. Accordion-fold or layer fabric (up to eight layers) and press. When possible, position templates so that outside edges of blocks or units will be on the straight grain. Hold the paper template in place or tape it to the fabric using a loop of transparent tape. Cut around the template with very sharp scissors, being sure to keep the blades of the scissors at a 90° angle to the fabric so all patches will be the same size. Folding the fabric will automatically produce reverse images of asymmetrical patches. If asymmetrical patches are needed without their reverse images, layer all fabric pieces right side up rather than folding.
3. An alternate method: Fold or layer the fabric as above. Make a plastic template including ¼″ seam allowance. Draw around the template with a pencil on the top layer of fabric. Pin the center of each patch and cut out with sharp scissors.

Rotary Cutter Method

1. For rotary cutting, begin by laying wrinkle-free, double-folded fabric on a cutting mat. Position it so the single fold and selvage are at the bottom and one raw, crossgrain edge is at the right. Using a see-through ruler marked with a right angle, match up the top edge of the ruler (or one of the right-angle lines) with the fold of the fabric. Cut the right edge of the fabric off, creating a straight edge from which to begin cutting strips. Swing mat and fabric around 180°. Position the ruler so that the marking for the desired strip width is even with the freshly cut edges of the fabric. Keep the top and bottom edges of fabric parallel to the horizontal lines of the ruler.

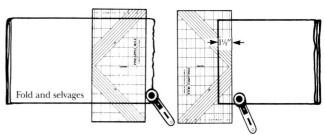

Fold and selvages

2. Squares can be cut from strips with the rotary cutter. Be sure to include ¼″ seam allowances all around (i.e., for 2″ finished patches cut the squares 2½″). Layer fabric up to eight layers for maximum speed in cutting.

3. Half-square triangles can be cut from strips with the rotary cutter also, but a formula for the correct added seam allowance must be applied. For example, for half-square triangles to fit next to 2″ finished squares in the same block, 2⅞″ squares are cut first, and then they are cut diagonally into half-square triangles. To figure for any size half-square triangle, simply add ⅞″ to the desired *finished* size using the measurement of the triangle on its short side.

4. Odd-sized and asymmetrical patches can be cut quickly with the rotary cutter by cutting around paper templates. Make sure templates include ¼″ seam allowance. Layer the fabric by accordion-folding (reverse image patches will automatically be cut) or stacking fabric pieces with right sides up (all pieces will be exactly the same with no reverse image patches). Tape templates to the top layer of fabric with a loop of transparent tape. When possible, position templates so that outside edges of blocks or units will be on the straight grain. Using a small rotary cutting ruler (1″ x 12″ or 6″ x 12″), rotary cut around the paper templates moving the ruler as needed.

MACHINE PIECING

1. Use a light neutral thread when sewing most fabrics, but use dark thread if all fabrics are dark. Pattern pieces include ¼″ seam allowance unless otherwise noted.

2. Place the pieces to be joined with the right sides together. Pin, matching seamlines, and sew with an accurate ¼″ seam allowance using a straight stitch, 10 to 12 stitches per inch. Press seam allowances to one side, toward the darker fabric, unless otherwise noted.

3. Chain-piece to save time and thread: Sew a seam and then immediately feed in a new set of pieces without lifting presser foot or clipping threads. Sew as many sets as possible in this manner, then clip them apart.

4. Where two seams meet, position one seam allowance in one direction and one seam allowance in the opposing direction. Butt the seams together exactly; they will hold each other in place. It is usually not necessary to pin.

5. When crossing triangular intersection seams, aim for the point where the seamlines intersect. This will avoid cutting off the points in the patchwork design.

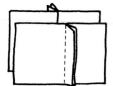 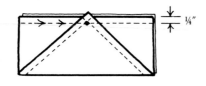

6. If one edge appears to be larger, put that side next to the feed dog of the machine so the extra will be eased into the seam without leaving tucks.

7. To piece the center of a block where eight points come together, begin by sewing four quarter blocks. Press seams as illustrated. Then sew quarters together to make half blocks. Press seam allowances of both halves in the same direction. When halves are placed right sides together, seams will fall in opposite directions. Match halves by butting seams together and aligning intersections. Pin, if necessary, and stitch.

8. To sew set-in pieces: (1) Stitch piece A to piece B right sides facing and raw edges even. Begin and end stitching ¼″ from each edge; backstitch at both beginning and end. (2) Sew C to A beginning and ending stitching ¼″ from each edge and backstitching as before. (3) Sew C to B beginning and ending stitching ¼″ from each edge and backstitching as before.

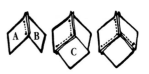

HAND PIECING

1. Make templates from patterns. *Do not* include seam allowances.

2. Draw exactly around templates on *wrong* side of fabric. Allow ½″ between templates and at least ¼″ from each edge of fabric. Mark corners clearly and accurately.

3. Cut pieces from fabric; cut ¼″ *outside* of marked line. Marked line is stitching line.

4. Place pieces right sides together matching and pinning at corners and intervals along marked lines. All pins should be placed at right angles to the marked sewing line. Remove the corner pin and insert the needle at this point. Take a stitch and then a small backstitch; then sew with a short, even running stitch checking from time to time that the marked lines on both front and back match. Remove pins as it becomes necessary. Sew to the end of marked line and backstitch. *Do not sew seam allowances down*; instead slide needle under seam allowances from point to point. This allows seam allowances to be pressed to either side. Assemble into units.

(Continued on page 89)

DOCUMENTING

Part of the joy of making a memory quilt can be documenting the experience for others to share. When you send invitations to friends asking for their help in making a memory quilt, it usually evokes warm and wonderful feelings. It seems they are more than willing to share in words some of their special remembrances about the people for whom the quilt is being made. A collection of these feelings is a delightful addition to the presentation of the memory quilt. In many cases, people have made scrapbooks enclosing the cards and letters that have accompanied the return of the quilt blocks. Each of these notes or messages has special meaning and contributes an extra touch to the "warm fuzzies" created by the quilt. A simple log kept by the project's organizer or the primary quiltmaker would be an interesting addition to a scrapbook. This scrapbook can be as simple or as complex as you like; it can be artistically organized or arranged very simply. A purchased scrapbook with plastic sleeves works very well because collected memorabilia can be easily inserted. If you are so inclined, you can make a fabric cover for the album to coordinate with the memory quilt. A photo transfer of the recipient or an extra block could be incorporated into the cover. The main point is that the album would provide extra memories for the person receiving the quilt.

Documentation of the quilt is also important because it is meaningful for future generations to know who made their family heirlooms. Time passes so quickly, and it is easy to lose track of who did what for whom and why. On page 28 we have designed a quilt label for your use and for inspiration. There are a number of ways to use this design. First of all, you could take a piece of white or light-colored fabric and trace over the design using a permanent marking pen or fabric paint. From there you simply need to fill in the appropriate information. Transfer pens, such as those described in the *Tools and Supplies* section, could also be used. However, in this case you would need to do a first tracing and then reverse that tracing in order to avoid having the label read backward. Because the transfer makes several copies, it can be a time-efficient method. It would work equally well to trace the quilt label design as shown in the book and then embroider it using thread to coordinate with the quilt.

Another option that is available is to incorporate the photo transfer process into the label. As you will notice, the label is designed to record information about the maker(s) and/or designer(s) as well as the recipient(s). Photos could first be placed in the appropriate boxes, and then a photo transfer could be made of the assembled quilt label. The meaning is significantly increased when one is able to see a picture of the person who has invested so much of her heart and soul in the stitching of the memories. Equally as important is a picture of the person who has evoked so much love and fondness that people were willing to spend their time and energy making a quilt filled with memories *especially* for him or her. If it is your choice to include a photo, simply copy the design onto a piece of white or cream-colored paper using the desired color of ink pen (ink does not have to be permanent since a photocopy of the design will be used to make the transfer). Be sure at this stage to include all of your specific information as this will also be included on the transferred label. Once you have written the information out on the paper, trace the area for the photo and use a small mat knife to cut out that area. Insert a photo behind this cut-out area and tape the photo into place. Have a color transfer made at a copy center as described in the section called *Personalizing*. The copier must have the capability for "mirror imaging" so your label will not transfer backward. If this process is not available to you locally, check the back of this book for mail order information on the photo transfer process.

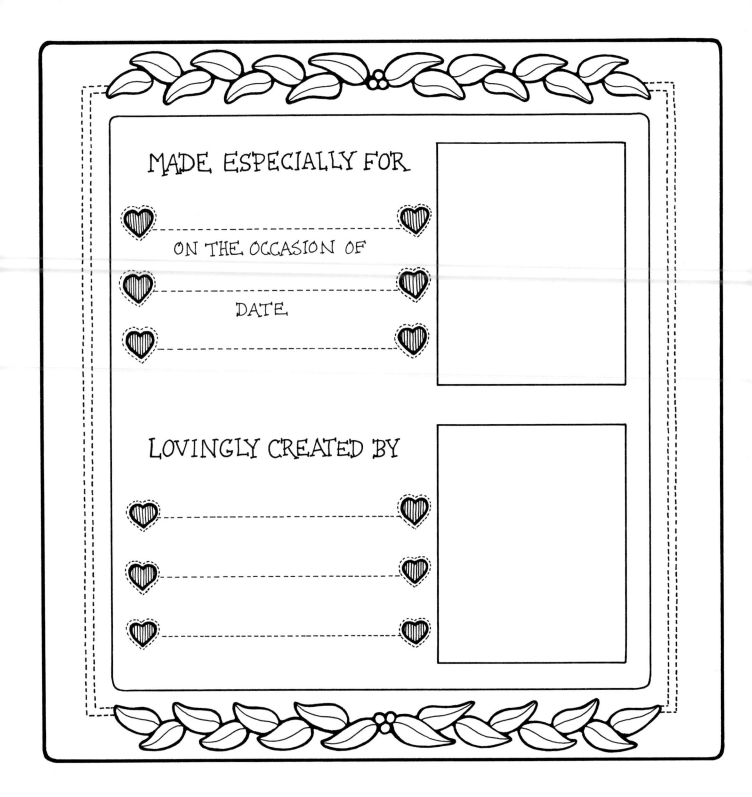

MADE ESPECIALLY FOR

ON THE OCCASION OF

DATE

LOVINGLY CREATED BY

Attaching labels to either the front or the back of the quilt provides a "secret pocket" for including some extra tidbits. The tiny, tucked-in treasures could be items or trinkets of special significance to the recipient; they could be scraps of fabric that in years to come could be used for patching or repairing the quilt should the need arise; the secret pocket could hold a message or prophesy for future generations - a quilted time capsule. Just remember that the labels and added touches are significant reminders of the warm memories that were inspiration for making the quilt in the first place. Make changes in the above label to fit your individual situation. The blank squares indicate suggested areas for photo transfers of the quiltmaker(s) or recipient(s).

WHAT HAPPENS IF...?

In this section we will propose several "problems" that might come up when you are working on a memory quilt. Many of these have come about from personal experience while helping our customers with their memory quilts. The more people participating, the more chance that these "problems" might arise. We put "problems" in quotation marks because sometimes "problems" become design changes and not "problems" at all. We have attempted to offer some possible solutions.

What happens if...

...the quilt is all put together, and someone sends in one more block?

Make the extra block into a matching pillow.

Applique it to the quilt back.

Piece it into the cover of a memory album.

...you only receive one-half the number of blocks you expected, and you were making a specific size?

Add sashing between the blocks to enlarge it.

Add alternate pieced or plain blocks between the memory blocks.

Set the blocks on point and add fill-in triangles.

Add borders.

...you end up with an uneven number of blocks?

Add a plain block or blocks that could be autographed.

Make the extra block or blocks that are needed yourself.

Make the uneven block or blocks into a wallhanging or pillow.

Applique or piece the uneven block or blocks to the back of the quilt.

Make a photo transfer of the giver and/or receiver and apply it to an extra block.

Place one to four extra blocks into the corners of the borders (see "Priscilla's 50th Birthday" on page 50).

...if you receive an ugly or outlandish block (the Cinderella block), a block with the wrong colors, or a block with very poor workmanship?

Redo the block yourself. We had to redo several Roman Stripe blocks in the "Friends" quilt because participants signed them on the wrong side of the block.

Put it in an inconspicuous place.

Request that it be remade.

If the colors are too bright, tea-dye it to tone it down.

Make it into a pillow.

Tell yourself it adds charm to the quilt.

...you want the quilt to be larger than you had planned?

Create double or triple sashings between the blocks (see the blocks on page 33 and the diagrams on page 30 for sashing ideas).

Alternate memory blocks with a simple pieced block, or choose a plain or print fabric for the alternate blocks.

Set the blocks on point and add fill-in triangles.

Add one or more borders.

...if the blocks are not the same size?

Trim all the blocks to the smallest size (this works best with applique blocks).

Add sashing strips around the small blocks to bring them up to the same size (see "This Is Your Life" on page 45).

Sort blocks according to size and stitch same-size blocks together adding borders between sizes (see "Friendship" on page 43).

Remake the blocks that just will not fit.

Add the larger blocks to the outside edges or to the corners so all four sides do not have to match.

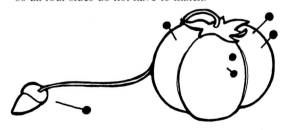

You will limit the possibility of these "problems" arising with careful organizing and planning, but because you are usually working with a great number of non-sewers, you can't eliminate them completely. As we stated before, these "problems" might become design changes, perhaps for the better. Be sure to make the directions as clear as possible, and even include an illustration. Refer the participants to the local quilt and fabric stores in their area and to any quilting groups. Also, don't forget to give them your phone number. Remember that questions asked during the design and construction phase may cut repair time later.

CARE OF A MEMORY QUILT

Enclose or attach a care label to the quilt. Unless you are sure of the permanency and washability of the products that were used to make and personalize a memory quilt, do not wash or dry-clean it. The best cleaning method would be a gentle vacuuming, or place it in your clothes dryer on air (no heat) for a short time. The best way to be sure that a quilt is washable is to prewash the fabric and do adequate testing of all techniques and products used.

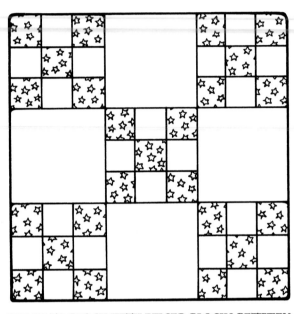

BLOCK TO BLOCK WITH PIECED BLOCKS BETWEEN

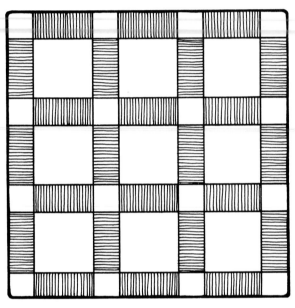

WITH SASHING STRIPS AND SETTING SQUARES

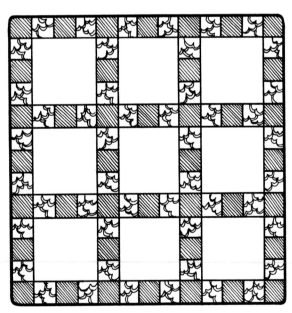

WITH PIECED SASHING

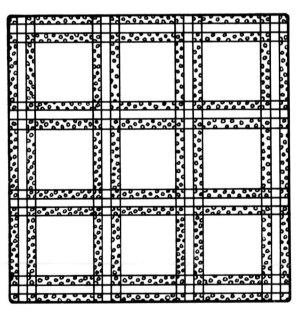

WITH TRIPLE SASHING

INSPIRATION

As we stated in the introductory section to the quilt patterns, this book is like no other in that regardless of which pattern is used, the number of friends and relatives that you involve in your friendship quilt will probably be very different than the number that we have planned for in our friendship quilts. As can be read under the photo captions accompanying each pattern, the possibilities for personalization are endless. The open areas in any quilt lend themselves to a myriad of uses, and you may have your own design preferences. Use the black-and-white quilt diagrams as a starting point in your explorations. The blocks that have children's drawings would work well with photo transfers or special messages written either in permanent marking pens or embroidery. Children's artwork could be substituted in any of the patterns shown with photo transfers. So many of the patterns in this book are interchangable in terms of techniques. Let your creativity run wild, and you will come up with numerous ideas of your own.

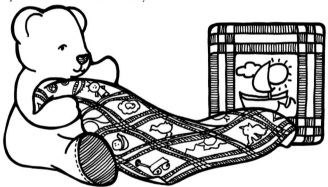

In the signature section we stated that you could iron freezer paper onto the back of white or muslin fabric and send pieces of it to friends for signatures. Squares are not the only shapes of fabric that can be sent. Rectangles would work, as would hearts, hands, stars, apples, hexagons, and flowers. These shapes can be hand or machine appliqued to the background. Full-size patterns for these shapes are found at the end of the pattern section. These are just a few suggestions for shapes that could be used. Children's coloring books are filled with simple shapes that could be used as a jumping off point for numerous other ideas. Be on the lookout for something that is appealing to you and would fit your particular memory quilt occasion.

The drawings below suggest several ways in which these or other simple shapes could be arranged. To do a random placement, begin by arranging the shapes on a large piece of background fabric or on smaller sections of fabric that have been stitched together. The stars in the design that is shown below could be clustered together rather than spread out. Simple embroidery or quilting lines radiating out from the star could represent shooting stars that might represent the shining stars of one's life. Play with the arrangement until it is pleasing to you, and then refer to the section on quiltmaking techniques for ways to apply them to the background fabric. In addition, this is an excellent way to plan a quilt when you do not know the number of participants involved. Stars could be spread apart or squeezed together depending on the number returned. Once the quilt is finished, it would not be difficult to add stars for those people who did not return their blocks on time. These extras could be applied to the back of the quilt as well as to the front by using hand applique or fusible webbing.

Feel free to experiment by combining designs that are found in this book (i.e., a section from one pattern may be adaptable for use with another pattern). The pattern for "Reading... The Key to Imagination", page 78, would be a good, basic block pattern for autographed hearts and hands. Use this simple block arrangement to suit your own needs.

An easy project would be to send a strip of fabric to your friends in a round-robin fashion. It would be simple and great fun to construct a quilt with these autographed strips. Your friends might enjoy playing off the comments of the previous signers. They could write or decorate as much or as little as they wanted. They could write about a shared memory, include a poem or a special saying, or say whatever they felt would be appropriate. We have included a few drawings to give you some visual images of how an idea like this might work.

One friend in Denver has taken the concept of "Guest Book" a step further. She has a patchwork tablecloth that she uses for special company. Within the patchwork there are alternate blocks of solid colors. When guests dine at her house, she asks the guests to sign their names and the date and add any extra comments they might have about the evening. The menu or a favorite recipe that is served could be added. Along this same line, on her guest bed she has a quilt to which she has added an extra strip of muslin. Any guest in her home who spends the night is invited to sign and date the quilt. What a loving and creative way to preserve the warm feelings that people have shared during a visit!

On pages 33 and 34 you will find a selection of quilt blocks. We have included these blocks for inspiration. The red-and-white squares frame different techniques. We made the center square 3″ so that it is perfect for a cropped snapshot. Any square can be bordered with a complimentary fabric. When placed side by side, the blocks create their own framework. For a scrappy effect, change the fabric on each side. Another idea is to divide the strips into an equal number of squares and stitch them to the block. This is an easy way to increase the size of the quilt without adding blocks. These simple blocks might inspire you to make a pillow, a small wallhanging, a doll quilt or some other wonderful small project with personalization techniques added to it to make a special memory. Quilts are not the only way to preserve memories, and it is often advantageous to think about smaller and quicker projects. Dinner with a friend or an invitation to a special party might inspire a hostess gift. A picture from years back would be fun to transfer onto fabric and make into a pillow. For a small investment in time and money, you would have a memorable gift. Not only would it be a remembrance from times past, but it would add to your collection of *new* memories!

SA-MAN. (Detail) Designed and stitched by Peggy Distretti Winfield for her daughter Samantha's high school graduation; 1990; Littleton, Colorado. This memory-evoking quilt contains photo transfers of school pictures. The remaining blocks were made by friends. The quilt's name comes from the shortened form of Samantha's name as it came back on school computer printouts through the years.

FRAMED SQUARES. Pictured above are suggestions for simple, easy-to-sew block designs that could utilize any of the techniques in the *Personalizing* section. Sashing width can be varied to increase or decrease the size of the quilt. Sashing strips also help to frame each individual block.

VARIATIONS OF "STARS AND STRIPES FOREVER". These four blocks show various color combinations that would work equally well for the "Stars and Stripes Forever" pattern pictured on page 83. The blocks made of solid fabrics could be signed in the large squares or in the centers of the stars. The rainbow block is signed in the clouds of the preprinted fabric. The red and green combination would be perfect for a signed tablecloth. The floral example could be signed in the sashing.

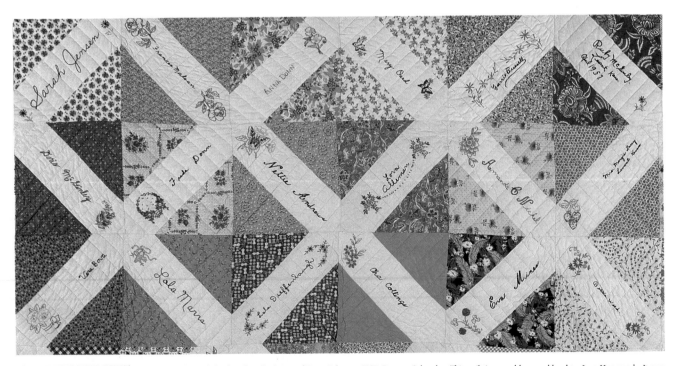

THE FRIENDSHIP QUILT. (Detail) Blocks made by friends and relatives of Grace Johnson; 1957; Denver, Colorado. This quilt is owned by granddaughter Jean Hammond. It was made for Grace Johnson in appreciation of her 40 years as a telephone operator. The beautiful embroidery was inspired by the print each participant used for the corners of her block.

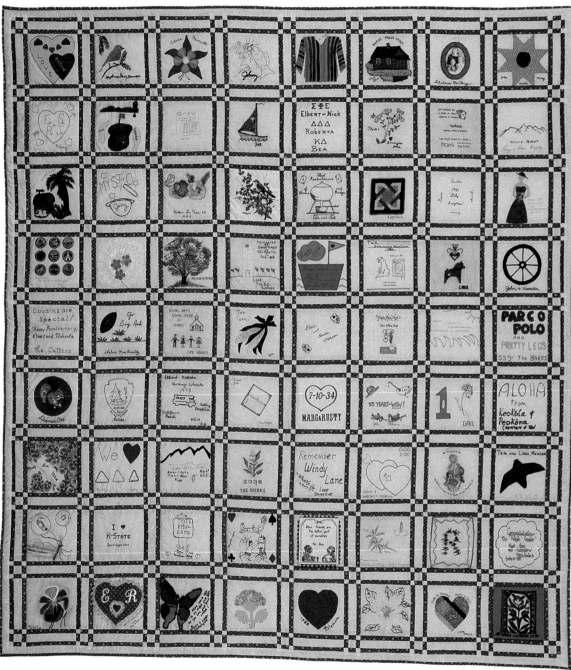

MEMORIES FOREVER. Designed by Nancy Smith and machine quilted by Sharon Holmes; 1989; Larned, Kansas; 80″ x 87″. Nancy involved friends and relatives throughout the country in a memory quilt for her in-laws, Elbert and Roberta Smith, who were celebrating their 55th wedding anniversary. She sent letters to over 80 friends on the Smiths' Christmas card list. Along with the letter outlining directions, she mailed a 7″ square of white fabric and a return envelope. Nancy recommended using a memory of the Smiths or a symbol or image that represented a shared experience. The 72 participants, men and women ranging in experience from novice to expert quilters, used a variety of techniques including cross stitch, marking pen, embroidery, photo transfers, iron-on fabrics, and applique. Along with the blocks came scores of letters and notes which Jack, the Smiths' son and Nancy's husband, organized into a scrapbook.

FRIDAY BLOCK PARTY CHRISTMAS QUILTS. The Friday Block Party quilting group of Littleton, Colorado, had a block exchange and challenge to complete a Christmas quilt within one year. Each member of the bee made 11 blocks using the same muslin background and Christmas reds and greens. They embroidered their names and then exchanged blocks.

CHRISTMAS FRIENDSHIP SAMPLER. Designed by Sherri B. Driver; 1988/90; Englewood, Colorado; 70″ x 70″. Being part of the block exchange was wonderful inspiration for Sherri. She has very young children and has a hard time finding large blocks of time to sew. She assembled the top on one of those rare days when her husband took the kids for the entire day. "I was taking the final stitches in the outer border when I heard the garage door open! Whew!"

FRIDAY BLOCK PARTY CHRISTMAS QUILT. Designed by Janet E. Robinson; 1988/90; Englewood, Colorado; 83″ x 83″. Janet wanted her quilt big enough for her queen size bed, so she had new members of the bee, who weren't in the original exchange, make a block for her, then she added a few special extras.

FRIDAY BLOCK PARTY CHRISTMAS QUILT. Designed by Karen Marie Nein; quilted by The Last Chance Quilters; 1989; Englewood, Colorado; 62″ x 77″. While making the house blocks within the Ohio Stars, her husband walked in and said, "Too bad you can't put a Christmas tree in the window." All of the Ohio Star blocks now have trees in the windows.

THE QUILT OF CHERISHED MEMORIES. (Detail) Designed by Donna Haffner and Violet McConnell for the 50th wedding anniversary of Ed and Erma Baldridge; 1985/86; Denver, Colorado. One detail shows a particularly meaningful block with special sayings, family jokes, phone numbers, cities, addresses, and dates associated with places they called home over the years.

GATHERED MEMORIES. Designed by Linda Gutin and stitched by Sharon Holmes for the 70th birthday celebration of Janice Cohen Gold, Linda's mother; 1991; Pikesville, Maryland; 50″ x 52″. The photo transfer process was used for this quilt. Linda states, "By the time an individual reaches age 70, there are few gifts that delight as much as a gathering of friends and memories. No doubt this quilt will be shared, handled, and cherished for the special moments and people remembered." Linda arranged each block of photos into a collage, representing different facets of her mother's life. Note the sashing strips and squares that form stars.

CHILD'S PRAYER QUILT. Designed by Kären L. Humphrey; 1989; Greenwood Village, Colorado; 86″ x 70″. This quilt was made for Kären's son Robert by his kindergarten class at Cherry Hills Christian School. "Each child made a self-portrait for it, and it helped the children develop friendships. Each child took the quilt home for one week during the school year to sleep with and pray for each of their friends." The blocks are colored with crayons that make transfers (paper to fabric), and the border is quilted with the handprints of the children.

ERIN'S QUILT. Designed and made for her granddaughter by Marjorie E. Kerr; 1980; Beatrice, Nebraska; 57″ x 57″. Marge made applique blocks by enlarging five-year-old Erin's drawings and artwork (see detail). She followed Erin's colors and added the three-dimensional features when possible. A portfolio of Erin's artwork accompanied the quilt.

FISHSCAPE. Blocks made by fourth graders at Weber Elementary School, Jefferson County, Colorado; assembled by Kathleen G. Emmel; 1991; Arvada, Colorado; 74″ x 74″. This class designed stylized fish and cut their own stencils. The stenciling was done under the direction of Cindy McConnell, art teacher. Using toothbrushes, Liquitex fabric paint was spattered onto the background muslin, creating a watercolor or transparent effect, then the fish were stenciled on top. Border pieces including seam allowances were precut for the children, but they did the actual machine piecing. An exciting part of the project for Kathy was that she received a grant of $1400 from Colorado Quilting Council, Inc. to purchase the sewing machines that the students used.

MEMORY QUILT. (Detail) Blocks made by the Knudson family and assembled by Tracy Philip for the 40th wedding anniversary of Eleanor and Jerry Knudson; 1991; Mandan, North Dakota. Some squares show family activities such as skating, sledding, and fishing, and the stenciled paper dolls represent the thirteen children. This detail also shows how to fit different size blocks together and still come out with a very unified look.

ARAPAHOE COUNTY QUILTERS PRESIDENT'S QUILT. Blocks made by members of ACQ for outgoing president, Barbara E. Lister; 1989/90; Englewood, Colorado; 60″ x 76″. Barb assembled the blocks using a black star print for sashing, and she added a creative touch, the red prairie point strip between the sashing and the border. Stars were quilted in the outside border to represent ACQs wonderful members. "It is really special, as each block is unique." The participants were given the size of the square and the black background fabric as guidelines. Just by seeing the blocks, Barb could identify many of the makers because each quilter's personality showed through.

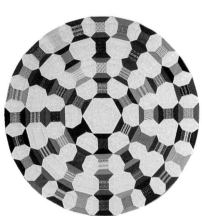

FRIDAY BLOCK PARTY SPOOLS QUILTS. The Friday Block Party quilting group of Littleton, Colorado, had a challenge for the setting of exchanged spool blocks which led to these friendship quilts. Each member chose five striped fabrics, made ten spools from each to exchange, and embroidered her name on one spool for each member.

SPOOL VEST. Designed by Diane Gasior Hienton; 1988; Westerville, Ohio. Diane says, "My 'no-time' schedule forced me to create something small and manageable. The vest was a great choice. Now I get to share this special piece with others as well as keep these fond memories close to my heart."

SPINNING SPOOLS. Designed by Janet E. Robinson; 1987/91; Englewood, Colorado; 39″ diameter. This was one of Janet's early piecing experiences. She chose a wonderfully creative way to assemble square blocks.

FRIENDSHIP SPOOLS. Designed by Mary (Sandy) Sanford; 1987/88; Littleton, Colorado; 26″ x 48″. "This quilt brings happy memories and is very special to me as several of its contributors have since moved away."

COLORADO FRIENDSHIP SPOOLS. Designed by DuAnn Wright; 1988; West Linn, Oregon; 45″ x 59″. DuAnn decided not to put all the spools in an orderly fashion; she used the signature spools to create movement in the quilt. Her greatest memory of this quilt was the wonderful quilting friends she made during the two years that she lived in Colorado.

SPOOLS OF WISDOM. Designed by Karen Marie Nein; 1988; Englewood, Colorado; 44″ x 51″. Karen made additional spools to enlarge the size of the quilt. Karen was inspired by friend and fellow group member, Sherri Driver, for the "loose-thread" idea, and Karen used the idea to embroider sayings along the inside border.

HANDFUL OF MEMORIES. Designed by Dee Brinley for Pamela E. Tillman; 1989; North Platte, Nebraska; 70″ x 84″. It is a remembrance of her days as a teacher at Willows Child Learning Center. The handprints are those of the children taught by Pam and were collected by her fellow teachers, totally unbeknownst to Pam. The buds on the vine surrounding the inscription are fingerprints of the children. The top was presented to Pam at the end of a quiltmaking lecture. Reasons for making quilts were discussed, "to be remembered" included. Pam was asked to "read" the quilt top to the class with tears and hugs resulting.

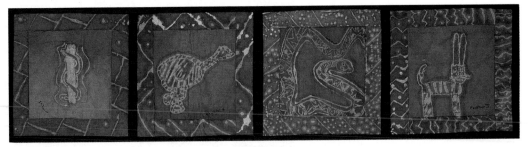

BATIK AFRICA. (Detail) Blocks made by fourth graders at Weber Elementary School, Jefferson County, Colorado; assembled by Kathleen G. Emmel; 1990; Arvada Colorado. Kathy's fourth grade classes have become known for the wonderful quilts they produce each year. In this particular case, after studying primitive African art, the students designed African animal motifs using paper and pencil. They transferred their designs onto 7½″ squares of muslin. The children used a cold water batik method to retrace their designs in wax. The fabric was dyed blue, wax was removed, strips were cut for framing each block, ¼″ seam allowances were marked on the wrong side, and finally the students hand sewed the strips to the blocks.

FLORENCE'S FRIENDSHIP QUILT. (Detail) Designed by Jean Jurgenson and Aileyn Ecob for their mother, Florence Renli; 1989; Canton, South Dakota. Jean and Aileyn wanted to give Florence's family and friends an opportunity to do something for her because she does so much for others. Some of the charm and beauty of this quilt is due to the wide latitude in the directions given to the quiltmakers. Jean and Aileyn received 70 blocks of every imaginable shape and size - truly a design challenge! By organizing the blocks into general size categories, cutting some of them down, and adding a little to others, they were able to organize them into this configuration.

VALENTINE MEMORIES. Sally has started a real tradition in her family. Each year for the past several years, she has made her husband a quilt for Valentine's Day. She says, "I make these quilts for my husband each year to show him how much I appreciate his love and support and encouragement all year long!" What a wonderful expression of love.

YOU HAVE STOLEN MY HEART. Designed and stitched by Sally Ann Collins; 1988; Walnut Creek, California; 25″ x 25″. The hearts are hand appliqued with silk fabric.

EMBROIDERED FEATHER HEART WREATH. Designed and stitched by Sally Ann Collins; 1989; Walnut Creek, California; 20″ x 20″. This is a magnificent example of Brazilian embroidery on a quilted feather heart wreath.

ALWAYS. Designed and stitched by Sally Ann Collins; 1991; Walnut Creek, California; 36″ x 36″. A wonderful mixture of piecing and applique, this wallhanging is available as a pattern. Contact *Special Treasures*, P.O. Box 30034, Walnut Creek, CA 94598, for more information.

43

FAMILY ALBUM. Designed and stitched by Gail P. Hunt; 1991; North Vancouver, British Columbia, Canada; 44″ x 56″. This quilt is an exciting use of the photo transfer process. The quilt incorporates different sizes of photos, making it unique. Antique fabrics were blended with new fabrics for the pieced stars. As an added and special element to this quilt, there is a large appliqued tree on the back with names of family members on the leaves. This is truly a wonderful example of the tying together of family memories.

OUR HOMES 1959-1989. Designed by Earl Scopel, stitched by Jean Scopel, and hand quilted by both; 1988/90; Evans, Colorado; 47″ x 32″. This quilt was made to commemorate the couple's 30th wedding anniversary and to create something uniquely theirs. "As my husband designed each block, he added to the house and environs at least one memory like the little red motor scooter he rode in Puerto Rico and the Yard of the Week sign in California. He pushed my abilities as machine appliquer to the limit! Planned, but not yet completed, are two small companion pieces, his childhood home, and my childhood home."

THIS IS YOUR LIFE. Designed and made by Susan Milstein; 1991; Montrose, Pennsylvania. This is a wonderful quilt made for Patti Bachelder, editor of *Quilting Today* magazine, to celebrate her 40th birthday. The unique thing about this quilt, aside from the photos that evoke such special memories, is the fact that the quilt incorporates pictures of all different sizes and shapes, each picture having its own frame. Photo by Steve Appel.

ALBUM. Designed and stitched by Terri Wiley; 1989; Aurora, Colorado; 24″ x 29″. This signature quilt was made as a Christmas present for Nancy Smith. All the employees at Great American Quilt Factory, Inc. drew names for a secret pal for the year; Terri drew Nancy's name and at the end of the year made this wonderful wallhanging for her. The signatures are those of the people connected with the business.

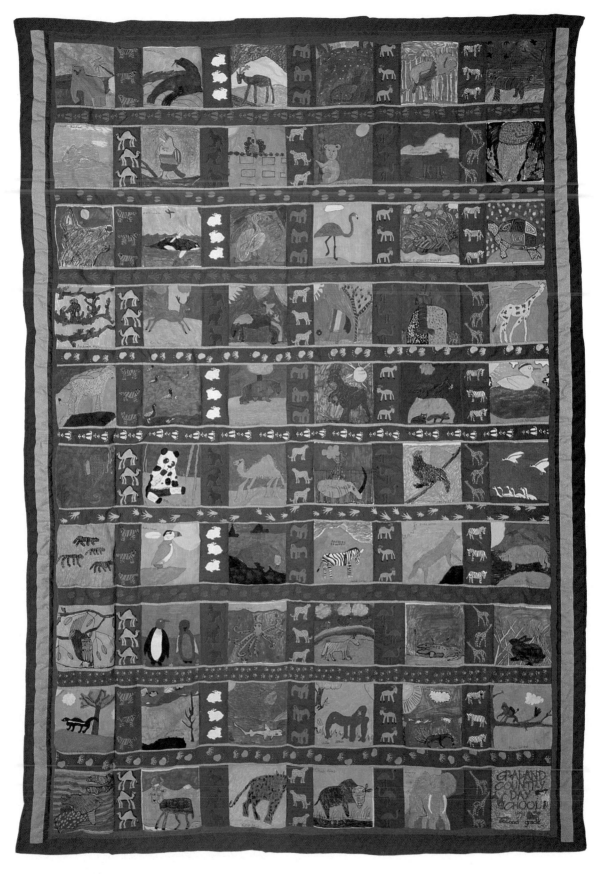

WILD ANIMALS. Blocks made by second graders, art teachers and parents at Graland Country Day School; coordinated by Cathy Kosal; 1990; Denver, Colorado; 74″ x 106″. For the past several years Cathy has organized a group quilt that has been used for a fundraising effort. Each year the techniques, as well as the designs, have become more elaborate. The students draw their designs onto paper first, then transfer them onto fabric, and finally color them using acrylic paints and permanent marking pens. The vertical sashing strips in this quilt are stenciled using reduced images from the actual blocks. The horizontal sashing strips are stenciled footprints.

WEDDING MEMORY. (Detail) Blocks made by friends and family of Mark and Denise Funk; 1985; Denver, Colorado. Participants were each asked to make one block representing a memory of the couple. The squares were assembled and presented as a surprise gift at the rehearsal dinner. The quilt was then hung at the wedding reception for all to see.

HEARTS. Blocks were made by members of the Bag Ladies, Parker, Colorado, for Katherine J. Nicklas; 1991; Elizabeth, Colorado; 45″ x 45″. Members of the group decided to make blocks to celebrate birthdays. Kathy wanted hearts, so she provided the pattern and specified pastel colors. (The pattern is from the book *A Celebration of Hearts* by Jean Wells and Marina Anderson, C & T Publishing, Lafayette, California, 1988.)

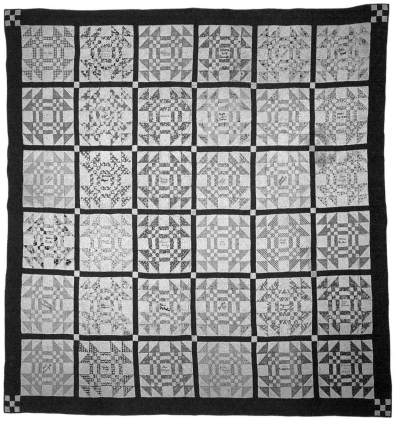

HOUSE BLOCKS. Designed and stitched by the Bag Ladies of Parker, Colorado, 1990. These were friendship blocks made for Virginia Gallup's 50th birthday. Virginia requested house blocks, and it is evident that creativity was in abundance. The word house conjured up all sorts of variations. The wonderful choice of fabrics added to the textural appearance of the blocks.

GOOSE IN THE POND. Made by ladies in the community of Lewis, Kansas; 75″ x 77″. The intended recipient and date are unknown. The quilt is owned by Terri Wiley of Aurora, Colorado. Terri states, "This quilt was a prop in our senior class play. When time came for everyone to take their things home, no one claimed this quilt. They were going to throw it away, but when I found my aunt's name on it, I decided to take it for her. She kept it for many years and then gave it to me when she found out my interest in quilts."

A TEA PARTY AT GRANDMA'S. Designed and stitched by Sherri B. Driver; 1988; Englewood, Colorado; 45″ x 54″. This quilt depicts Sherri's memories of her grandmother, Jeanette Allen McNair-Bain. It includes things found in trunks at her house, a porcelain doll she won in a raffle in the 1940s, and Sherri's father's old teddy bear. The fabrics were her grandmother's, gleaned from her scrap bag or snipped from dresses that her grandmother had worn. Raggedy Anne's dress was cut from her grandmother's curler cap. Making this quilt was therapy for Sherri to help her through the death of her grandmother. The quilt was a state runnerup in the Childhood Memories contest sponsored by the Museum of American Folk Art.

FLOWER STUDY. (Detail) Blocks made by first graders at Normandy Elementary School, Jefferson County, Colorado; assembled by Mary Christofferson; 1990; Littleton, Colorado. This quilt was made in early spring as part of a drawing unit in which students studied flowers and lines. Fabric crayons were used to transfer the children's drawings onto the cloth background. The quilt is now a happy retirement memory for Mary.

COVELL ANNIVERSARY QUILT. (Detail) Designed and stitched by Osie Covell Lebowitz for her parents' 47th wedding anniversary; 1990; Frederick, Maryland. The simplified body shapes were machine pieced, appliqued and quilted with additional surface embellishments using yarn, embroidery floss, beads, buttons, and permanent marking pens for facial features and written details including names and dates.

AGGIELAND. (Detail) Designed and stitched by Kathi Lamkin for her son Bob when he graduated from Texas A & M; 1989; Aurora, Colorado. The traditional Log Cabin pattern is used beautifully in this quilt. The cross-stitched centers of the blocks include school symbols and sayings. Kathi states, "The real challenge was stenciling names, dates, special events, and school seals on the borders to quilt two months before graduation."

STRIPED STARS. Designed by Judith A. Kraus; 1988; Littleton, Colorado; 50″ x 50″. The individual blocks were pieced by 25 members of the Night Owls Quilting Bee of Vienna, Virginia, and Judy was the lucky winner of the blocks in a drawing. "This was the first time some of us had used stripes in a block. I was surprised and pleased that no stripe was repeated."

PRISCILLA'S 50TH BIRTHDAY. Designed by Marinda Brown Stewart for Priscilla Miller; 1988; West Cornwall, Connecticut; 98″ x 109″. Individual blocks were made by friends throughout the fabric industry. A wide variety of fabrics and techniques were used. There are sixty total squares, and Priscilla says, "Each one brings a flood of memories." The addition of the four blocks that are sewn into the corners of the border is a very creative way to add extra or late blocks. The techniques and styles used in many cases gave Priscilla clues as to the designer.

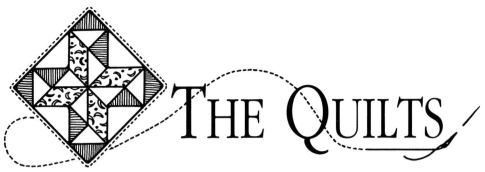

THE QUILTS

The quilts that follow have been chosen for many reasons. We wanted to bring you a broad spectrum of memory quilts with a wide variety of personalization techniques. The making of the quilts can be done entirely by one person or involve any number of participants. Some would be easy to make into kits with all the fabric choices made in advance; others are charming scrap quilts. Below each quilt is a description of the quilt, names of the makers, the reason for making the quilt, and perhaps most important, "other suggested uses". We want your creativity to soar! Personalize each quilt in your own way. Read through the book for the many suggestions and ideas we present, but don't stop there. The only reason we stopped is because we had to get this book into print sometime, but our creative juices are still flowing.

Each of the following quilts is set up in basically the same way. All of the quilts can be expanded to allow for more blocks or reduced in size to include fewer blocks. If the size is changed, adjust the yardage accordingly. When applicable, directions are given for traditional as well as quick piecing techniques.

At the bottom of each photo, we have listed other suggested ways to make the quilt. Any of these quilts could be personalized with one or another of several techniques.

Refer to *Quiltmaking Techniques* for help with specific methods. Refer to *Personalizing* for specific personalization methods. Please read the charts and directions thoroughly before purchasing or cutting fabric.

Because of fabric shrinkage, cutting techniques and individual cutting discrepancies, the yardage for these quilts has been adjusted upward. It is always a good idea to cut the entire quilt as soon as possible so that more fabric can be purchased if necessary. Extra fabric is included for quilts with mitered borders. Pieced block, setting square, border, and binding yardages have been listed separately to allow for individual fabric choices. When the quilt width is close to 45", we have listed two different yardages for quilt backing. If you plan to prewash your fabric, you will probably need to go with the greater amount. Quilt measurements are given width by length. Measure *your* quilt before cutting borders. Check quilt diagrams to see which border to stitch on first. Metric measurements (in parentheses) have been slightly rounded for your convenience.

Personalizing - The directions do not usually specify when to personalize your quilt. It is generally easier and sometimes necessary to personalize the blocks before they are put together. For example, if you are incorporating photo transfers, they need to be applied to the fabric before the blocks are made. Written signatures, on the other hand, can be applied even after the quilt has been quilted. Many times, depending on the occasion, you may want to have the finished quilt to give to the recipient at a celebration. Part of the celebration (i.e., wedding reception, baby shower) may be for the guests to sign the quilt. Embroidered designs and signatures can be done at any point up until the quilt is basted to the backing and batting. Painting, coloring, and stenciling are most easily and cleanly done before the blocks are put together. In short, the time for doing the personalization depends on the personalization technique you have chosen as well as your method of organizing the project.

FINISHING STEPS FOR ALL QUILTS
See *Quiltmaking Techniques,* page 25, and *Personalizing,* page 18, for more detailed descriptions.
1. Press quilt top well.
2. Mark for quilting if desired.
3. If necessary (depending on size), piece backing. All backings that require piecing, except for *Friends*, are pieced horizontally to save fabric.
4. Piece batting if necessary.
5. Layer backing, batting and quilt top; baste.
6. Quilt by hand or machine, or tie.
7. Bind quilt.

APPLES FOR THE TEACHER

APPROXIMATE FINISHED SIZE 66" x 78"

6" BLOCK - 32 pieced blocks alternating with 31 apple-stenciled blocks set 7 x 9

SETTING - Blocks set straight.

TECHNIQUE - Patchwork, fabric stenciling, and fine permanent marking pen.

Yardage (42"- 45" or 107-114 cm wide):

Pieced blocks

Muslin	¾ yd. (.7 m)
Darks to total	⅞ yd. (.8 m)
Setting blocks (muslin)	1¼ yds. (1.2 m)
Border 1	⅓ yd. (.3 m)
Border 2	1⅞ yd. (1.8 m)
Border 3	½ yd. (.5 m)
Border 4	¾ yd. (.7 m)
Binding	¾ yd. (.7)
Backing	4¼ yds. (3.9 m)
Batting (packaged)	72" x 90" (180 cm x 225 cm)
Batting (45" wide)	4 yds. (3.7 m)

Cutting (Refer to *Cutting For Machine Piecing*, page 25):

Choose Traditional *or* Strip Piecing Method.

Traditional Method

Muslin	128 - Template B (2½" x 2½")
	31 - Template A (6½" x 6½")
Darks	160 - Template B (2½" x 2½")
Border 1	5 crossgrain cuts 1½" wide
Border 2	6 crossgrain cuts 8½" wide
Border 3	8 crossgrain cuts 1½" wide
Border 4	8 crossgrain cuts 2½" wide
Binding	8 crossgrain cuts 2½" wide

Strip Piecing Method

Muslin	31 - pieces 6½" x 6½"
	8 crossgrain cuts 2½" wide
Darks	10 crossgrain cuts 2½" wide
Borders	as above
Binding	as above

Traditional Method

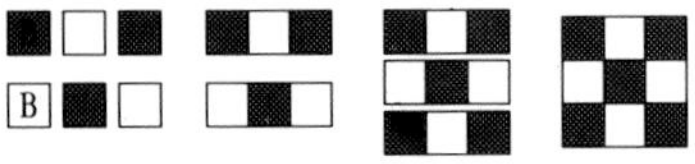

Strip Piecing Method

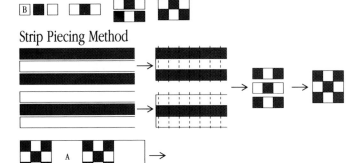

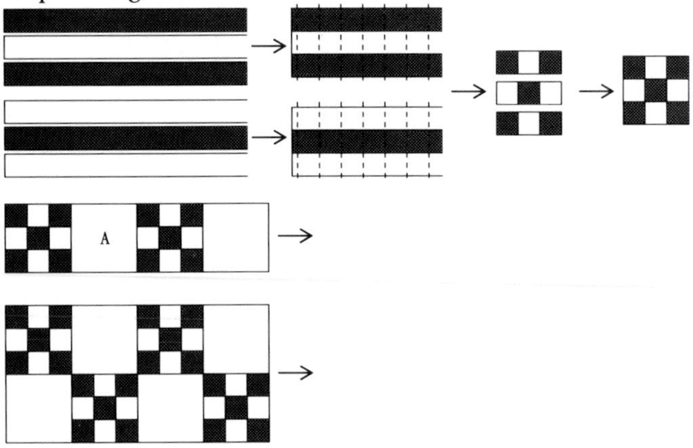

Directions:

Use ¼" seam allowances throughout. Refer to *Quiltmaking Techniques*, page 25, for specific sewing methods. Refer to quilt diagram, color photo and piecing diagrams for order of assembling. Refer to page 21 for stenciling techniques.

1. Traditional Method: Piece 32 9-patch blocks following diagram. Press.

2. Strip Piecing Method: Following diagrams, make 2 muslin-dark-muslin strip sets, press seams toward darks, and cut 32 segments 2½" wide. Make 4 dark-muslin-dark strip sets, press seams toward darks, and cut 64 segments 2½" wide. Assemble and sew segments into blocks following diagram. Press.

3. Prepare apple-stenciled blocks. Apple and house stencil patterns are on page 101.

4. Sew 9 horizontal rows alternating 9-patch blocks with apple blocks. Odd rows begin with a 9-patch, and even rows begin with an apple block.

5. Sew alternating rows together following diagram.

6. For borders, follow cutting directions above and refer to *Stairstep Borders* section of *Quiltmaking Techniques*, page 90. Sew borders to quilt sides first, then top and bottom. Note: Prepare needed lengths for house border, then stencil, then sew to quilt.

7. Refer to *Finishing Steps For All Quilts*, page 51. Quilt is hand quilted around stencils and ¼" from seams in 9-patch blocks. Trees are hand quilted between houses (pattern on page 101).

APPLES FOR THE TEACHER. Blocks made by fouth graders at Weber Elementary School, Jefferson County, Colorado; assembled by Kathleen G. Emmel; 1987; 66″ x 78″. For the past several years, Kathy has helped her fourth graders make a quilt. She incorporates many subjects into this process, including a geometry unit. For the "Apples for the Teacher" quilt, each child was given a kit with a full diagram of the proposed quilt and specific directions for making their part. The fabrics were precut, and sewing lines were premarked. Each child sewed his or her own nine-patch block, stenciled an apple block, and signed his or her name to each. Kathy added the borders, and the children stenciled the schoolhouses. Kathy machine quilted and bound the quilt. The children were incredibly proud. The hardest part for the kids? Tying the knots in the thread!

Other suggested uses: The 6½″ squares can be used for any applique or photo transfers. The nine-patch can be done in the same color or in scraps of the same color which will help to create a more pulled-together look if your 6½″ blocks are different. Other patterns could be used for stenciling such as a heart or a hand.

BLUE FRIENDSHIP BLOCKS

APPROXIMATE FINISHED SIZE 30″ x 30″
6″ BLOCK - 25 blocks set 5 x 5
SETTING - Blocks set straight.
TECHNIQUE - Patchwork with hand embroidery, stenciling, and permanent marking pen.

Yardage (42″- 45″ or 107-114 cm wide):
Blocks
Muslin	¼ yd. (.3 m)	
Blue scraps - lights,mediums and darks to total	2 yds. (1.9 m)	
Accent scraps to total	⅛ yd. (.2 m)	
Binding	⅜ yd. (.4 m)	
Backing	1 yd. (1 m)	
Batting (packaged)	45″ x 60″ (112.5 cm x 150 cm)	
Batting (45″ wide)	1 yd. (1 m)	

Cutting (Refer to *Cutting For Machine Piecing*, page 25):
Participants were asked to make a block using blue prints. Some added an accent color to their blocks which helps to break the repetition.
Choose Traditional *or* Strip Piecing Method.
Traditional Method - For each block, cut:

Center	
Muslin	1 - Template A
Blue scraps or accent color	2 - Template B
Middle triangles	
Blue scraps	4 - Template B
Outer triangles	
Blue scraps	4 - Template A
Binding	3 crossgrain cuts 2½″ wide

Pineapple Rule Method - For each block cut:

Center	
Muslin	1 - Template A
Blue scraps or accent color	2 - Template B
Middle triangles	
Blue scraps	4 - Rectangles 2¼″ x 3½″
Outer triangles	
Blue scraps	4 - Rectangles 2¾″ x 4¾″
Binding	as above

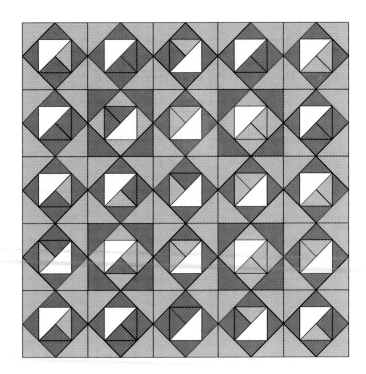

Pineapple Rule Method

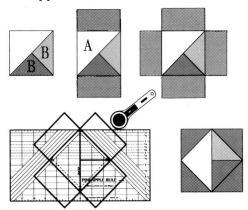

Traditional Method

Directions:

Use ¼″ seam allowances throughout. Refer to *Quiltmaking Techniques*, page 25, for specific sewing methods. Refer to quilt diagram, color photo and piecing diagrams for order of assembling. Refer to pages 18 and 20 for embroidery and personalization techniques.

1. Traditional Method: Sew 2 B triangles together. Make 25. Add signature triangle A to form squares. Add 4 B triangles to each square. Add 4 A triangles to each square. Press blocks.

2. Pineapple Rule Method: Sew 2 B triangles together. Make 25. Add signature triangle A to form squares. Sew 2¼″ x 3½″ rectangles around each A square as illustrated. Press seams toward rectangles. Place Pineapple Rule on wrong side of block with 45° angles following stitching lines. The center

(Continued on page 88)

BLUE FRIENDSHIP BLOCKS. Blocks made by members of the Night Owls Quilting Bee in Vienna, Virginia for Judy Kraus; assembled by Judy; 1989; Littleton, Colorado; 30″ x 30″. Judy says that the Night Owls taught her almost everything she knows about quilting, and when she moved away, they made these blocks for her. The blocks contain special messages and embellishments.

Other suggested uses: The signature triangle could be used equally well for photo transfers, small drawings using fine-point marking pens, or embroidery. This is an easy block for new quilters to make. A kit would be easy to assemble.

DEAR AMELIA

APPROXIMATE FINISHED SIZE 29″ x 33″
4¼″ BLOCK - 30 blocks set 5 x 6
SETTING - Blocks set straight.
TECHNIQUE - Patchwork with fine permanent marking pen.

Yardage (42″- 45″ or 107-114 cm wide):
Block
Muslin	½ yd. (.5 m)
Medium prints to total	⅞ yd. (.8 m)
Dark prints to total	⅝ yd. (.6 m)
Border 1	¼ yd. (.3 m)
Border 2	½ yd. (.5 m)
Binding	⅜ yd. (.4 m)
Backing	1 yd. (1 m)
Batting (packaged)	45″ x 60″ (112.5 cm x 150 cm)
Batting (45″ wide)	1 yd. (1 m)

Cutting (Refer to *Cutting For Machine Piecing*, page 25):
Choose Traditional *or* Strip Piecing Method.
Traditional Method
Muslin	30 - Template A (3½″ x 3½″)
Mediums	120 - Template C
Darks	120 - Template B
Border 1	4 crossgrain cuts 1¼″ wide
Border 2	4 crossgrain cuts 3¾″ wide
Binding	4 crossgrain cuts 2½″ wide

Strip Piecing Method
Muslin	30 - pieces 3½″ x 3½″
Mediums	14 crossgrain cuts 1¾″ wide
Darks	7 crossgrain cuts 2″ wide
Borders	as above
Binding	as above

Traditional Method

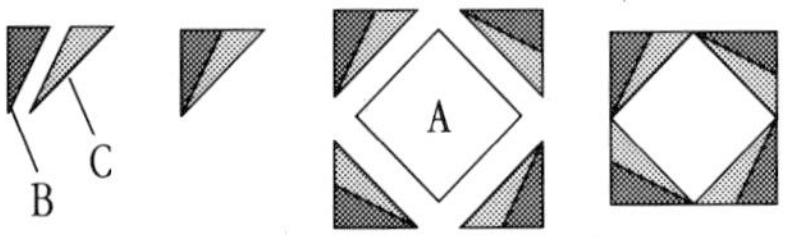

Strip Piecing Method

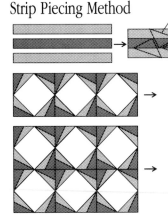

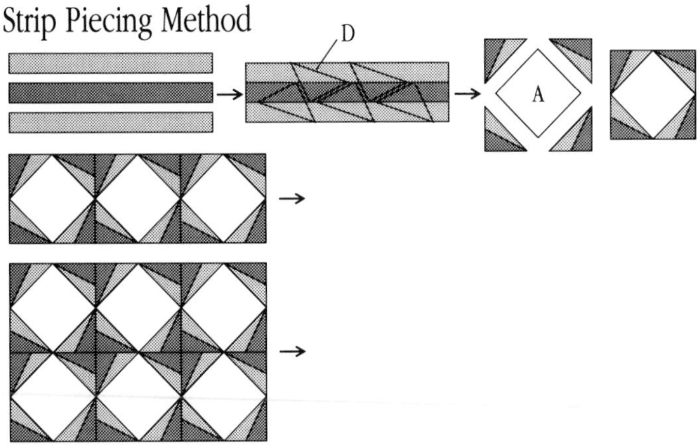

Directions:

Use ¼″ seam allowances throughout. Refer to *Quiltmaking Techniques*, page 25, for specific sewing methods. Refer to quilt diagram, color photo and piecing diagrams for order of assembling. Refer to page 18 for personalization techniques.

1. Traditional Method: Sew B to C to make 120 B/C units. Sew B/C units to A. Make 30 blocks. Press seams toward outside edges of blocks.

2. Strip Piecing Method: Make 7 medium-dark-medium strip sets. Press seams toward dark strip. Make Template D of plastic; transfer gray line to plastic. Lay plastic template on right side of strip set, matching gray line on template to seamline on strip set as shown. Draw around template. Slide template to next position shown (keep same side up for marking all pieces), and draw around it again. Continue to end of strip. Cut out. Sew D units to A. Make 30 blocks. Press seams toward outside edges of blocks.

3. Sew blocks together into 6 horizontal rows of 5 blocks each.

4. Sew rows together.

5. For mitered borders, follow cutting directions above and refer to *Mitered Borders* section of *Quiltmaking Techniques*, page 90.

6. Refer to *Finishing Steps For All Quilts*, page 51. Quilt is machine quilted in horizontal, vertical, and diagonal lines between patches; between borders; and in parallel lines the width of the sewing machine foot in the wide floral border.

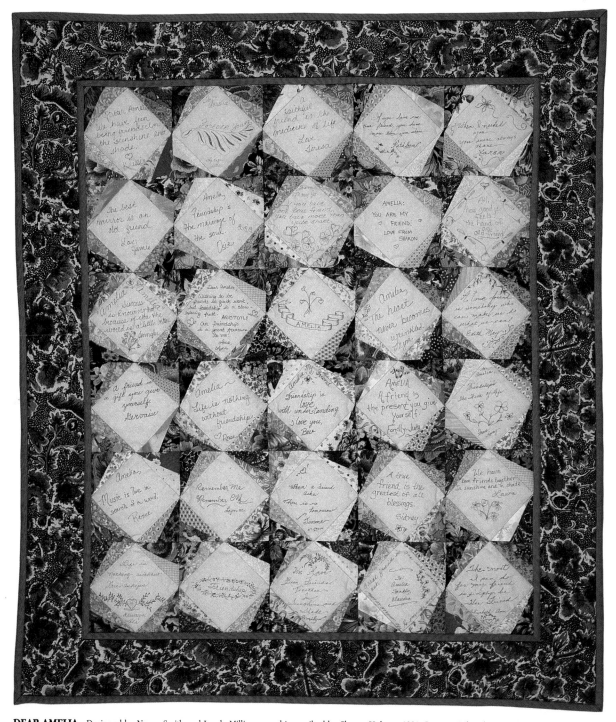

DEAR AMELIA. Designed by Nancy Smith and Lynda Milligan; machine quilted by Sharon Holmes; 1991; Denver, Colorado; 29″ x 33″. We chose to sign the muslin squares with old-fashioned sayings and drawings. The beauty of this quilt is that although it may look difficult to piece, it is actually easy, and we have presented two methods for you to try. Be sure to keep a contrast between the two corner fabrics, or you will lose the pinwheel that is created.
Other suggested uses: The solid squares of muslin can be used for photo transfers, tiny drawings, embroideries, appliques, or simple signatures.

FAMILY TIES

APPROXIMATE FINISHED SIZE 55″ x 61″
6″ BLOCK - 72 blocks set 8 x 9
SETTING - Blocks set straight but in alternating directions.
TECHNIQUE - Patchwork and permanent marking pen.

Yardage (42″- 45″ or 107-114 cm wide):
Blocks

Cream stripe	1¾ yds. (1.6 m)
Mediums to total	1⅜ yds. (1.3 m)
Darks to total	1⅛ yds. (1.1 m)
Border (cream stripe)	2 yds. (1.9 m)
	(1 yd. or 1 m if not a stripe)
Binding (bias-cut stripe)	1 yd. (1 m)
	(⅝ yd. or .6 m if not a stripe)
Backing	3⅜ yds. (3.1 m)
Batting (packaged)	72″ x 90″ (180 cm x 225 cm)
Batting (45″ wide)	3⅓ yds. (3.1 m)

Cutting (Refer to *Cutting For Machine Piecing*, page 25):

Cream stripe	72 - Template A
Mediums	144 - Template C
Darks	288 - Template B
Border (stripe)	2 - pieces 4″ x 58″
	2 - pieces 4″ x 64″
	(7 crossgrain cuts if not a stripe)
Binding (optional bias-cut stripe)	prepared to 2½″ x 240″
	(6 crossgrain cuts 2½″ wide
	if not a stripe)

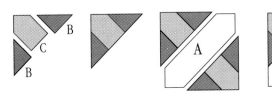

Directions:

Use ¼″ seam allowances throughout. Refer to *Quiltmaking Techniques*, page 25, for specific sewing methods. Refer to quilt diagram, color photo and piecing diagrams for order of assembling. Refer to page 18 for personalization techniques.

1. Sew B to each side of C to make 144 B/C units. Sew B/C units to each side of A. See diagram. Press.
2. Sew 9 horizontal rows of 8 blocks each, alternating direction of block as shown. Note that first block of each row also alternates direction.
3. Sew rows together, taking care with alternating directions of blocks.
4. For mitered border, follow cutting directions above and refer to *Mitered Borders* section of *Quiltmaking Techniques*, page 90, for joining it to the quilt.
5. Refer to *Finishing Steps For All Quilts*, page 51. Binding for this quilt was cut on the bias to utilize the striped fabric. Quilt is hand quilted ¼″ from B/C unit seams and A seams.

FAMILY TIES. Designed and made by Sandee Wachal; 1988; Colorado Springs, Colorado; 55″ x 61″. Sandee moved from Minnesota over 22 years ago. For her grandmother's 87th birthday celebration and family reunion in Minnesota, Sandee made an autograph quilt to take back with her. The individual blocks were easy to sew. Sandee very cleverly used a white-on-white striped fabric for the diagonal strip through the block which helped those autographing the quilt to sign in the middle. Family members signed their names, where they were from, and the year. Sandee says that when she gets homesick, she bundles up in the quilt for comfort.

Other suggested uses: This is a great quilt pattern to send out to friends to make. Let them choose their own fabrics (give them guidelines if you want to stay with a certain color scheme), sign the blocks, and return them. The diagonal strips allow plenty of room for inspiring thoughts.

FRIENDS

APPROXIMATE FINISHED SIZE 71″ x 83″
3″ BLOCK - 396 blocks set 18 x 22
SETTING - Blocks set straight but in alternating directions.
TECHNIQUE - Patchwork and fine permanent marking pen.

Yardage (42″- 45″ or 107-114 cm wide):
Blocks
Muslin	1¾ yds. (1.6 m)
Darks to total	3¼ yds. (3 m)
Border 1	½ yd. (.5 m)
Border 2	2 yds. (1.9 m) (2⅝ yds.or 2.4 m of a 4-repeat stripe)
Binding	¾ yd. (.7 m)
Backing	5⅛ yds. (4.7 m)
Batting (packaged)	81″ x 96″ (202.5 cm x 240 cm)
Batting (45″ wide)	4⅓ yds. (4 m)

Cutting (Refer to *Cutting For Machine Piecing*, page 25):
Choose Traditional *or* Strip Piecing Method.
Traditional Method
Muslin	396 - Template A (1½″ x 3½″)
Darks	792 - Template A (1½″ x 3½″)
Border 1	8 crossgrain cuts 1½″ wide
Border 2	8 crossgrain cuts 8″ wide
	(or 4 lengthwise cuts 8″ wide of a stripe)
Binding	8 crossgrain cuts 2½″ wide

Strip Piecing Method
Muslin	36 crossgrain cuts 1½″ wide
Darks	72 crossgrain cuts 1½″ wide
Borders	as above
Binding	as above

Traditional Method

Strip Piecing Method

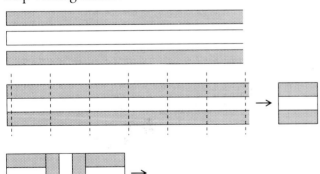

Directions:

Use ¼″ seam allowances throughout. Refer to *Quiltmaking Techniques*, page 25, for specific sewing methods. Refer to quilt diagram, color photo and piecing diagrams for order of assembling. Refer to page 18 for personalization techniques.

1. Traditional Method: Piece 396 blocks following diagram. Press.
2. Strip Piecing Method: Make 36 dark-muslin-dark strip sets, press seams toward darks, and cut them into 396 segments 3½″ wide. See diagram.
3. Sew 22 horizontal rows of 18 blocks each alternating direction of blocks.
4. For mitered borders, follow cutting directions above and refer to *Mitered Borders* section of *Quiltmaking Techniques*, page 90, for joining them to the quilt.
5. Refer to *Finishing Steps For All Quilts*, page 51. Quilt is machine quilted in the ditch between blocks, between borders, and between stripes in the wide outer border.

FRIENDS. Designed and made by Nancy Smith and Lynda Milligan; machine quilted by Sharon Holmes; 1989; Denver, Colorado; 71″ x 83″. This was a celebration gift for a special friend of ours, Jean Yancey. Jean, a long-time supporter of women in business and a personal mentor of ours, was celebrating her 75th birthday. We obtained a list of the invitees to Jean's birthday party and sent each of them a pieced Roman Stripe block. We asked that they sign their names and any personal messages and return the blocks to us. Unsigned blocks were also included in the quilt to be signed at the party, and for friends, as yet unmet, to sign in the future. Thus the quilt has become a living legacy as well as a past tribute. As time has gone by, the inner border has also become filled with signatures.

Other suggested uses: Because this block is so simple to piece, it is a good quilt to make for a baby or bridal shower. Include extra unsigned blocks to be signed at the actual celebration.

GEMSTONES

APPROXIMATE FINISHED SIZE 44″ x 52″
4¼″ BLOCK - 80 blocks set 8 x 10
SETTING - Blocks set straight.
TECHNIQUE - Patchwork and hand embroidery.

Yardage (42″- 45″ or 107-114 cm wide):
Blocks

Solids to total	1 yd. (1 m)
Prints to total	1¼ yds. (1.2 m) (2⅛ yds. or 2 m if using Pineapple Rule method)
Border	1⅛ yds. (1.1 m)
Binding	½ yd. (.5 m)
Backing	2⅞ yds. (2.7 m)
Batting (packaged)	45″ x 60″ (112.5 cm x 150 cm)
Batting (45″ wide)	1⅝ yds. (1.5 m)

Cutting (Refer to *Cutting For Machine Piecing*, page 25):
Choose Traditional *or* Strip Piecing Method.
Traditional Method

Solids	80 -	Template A (3½″ x 3½″)
Prints	320 -	Template B
Border	5 crossgrain cuts 5½″ wide	
Binding	5 crossgrain cuts 2½″ wide	

Pineapple Rule Method

Solids	80 -	squares 3½″ x 3½″
Prints	320 -	rectangles 2¼″ x 3½″
Border	as above	
Binding	as above	

Traditional Method

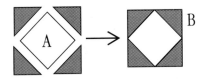

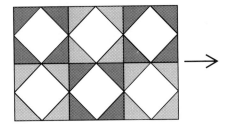

Pineapple Rule Method

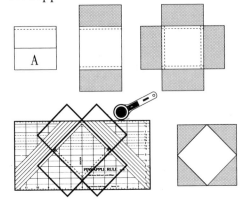

Directions:

Use ¼″ seam allowances throughout. Refer to *Quiltmaking Techniques*, page 25, for specific sewing methods. Refer to quilt diagram, color photo and piecing diagrams for order of assembling. Refer to page 20 for embroidery techniques.

1. Traditional Method: Sew 4 B triangles to each A square. Press seams toward outer edges of blocks.
2. Pineapple Rule Method: Sew 2¼″ x 3½″ rectangles around each A square as illustrated. Press seams toward rectangles. Place Pineapple Rule on wrong side of block with 45° angles following stitching lines. The center vertical line on the ruler should line up point to point across the square. Using rotary cutter, trim off corners as shown. Repeat for other 3 sides of each block.

(Continued on page 88)

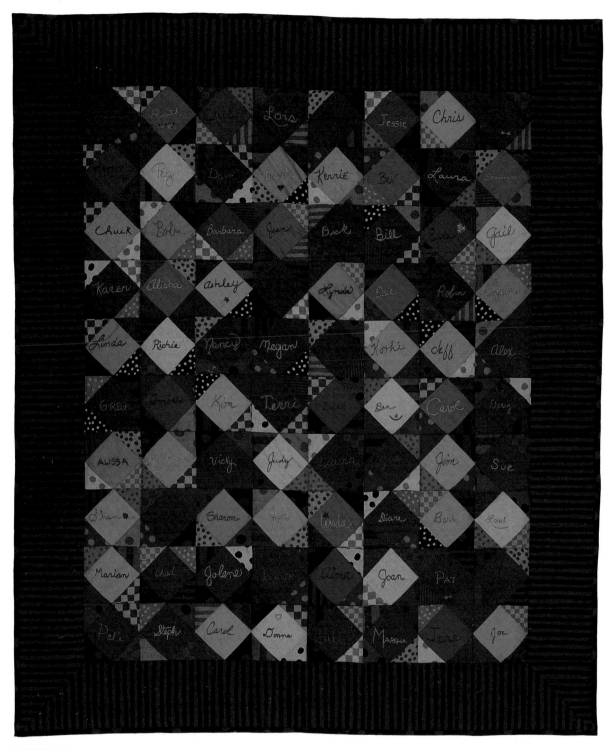

GEMSTONES. Designed by Nancy Smith and Lynda Milligan; machine quilted by Sharon Holmes; 1991; Denver, Colorado; 44″ x 52″. Simple, fun, easy, and quick would all describe this quilt. We have chosen an array of bright and bold prints from a collection of fabrics called *Color Parade* by P & B Fabrics to give this quilt the sparkle of jewels. All of the signatures have been embroidered in coordinating, bright threads. Directions are given for traditional sewing methods as well as the quick *Pineapple Rule* method.

Other suggested uses: Choose from photo transfers in the squares, counted cross stitch signatures over waste canvas, small drawings of faces or flowers.

GENTLE TIMES

APPROXIMATE FINISHED SIZE 50" x 67"
6" BLOCK - 59 blocks (whole) set 5 x 7 on point
SETTING - Blocks set on point with half and quarter blocks at the outside edge.
TECHNIQUE - Patchwork.

Yardage (42"- 45" or 107-114 cm wide):
Blocks

Muslin	3 yds. (2.8 m)	
Pastels to total	2¼ yds. (2.1 m)	
Border	1⅛ yds. (1.1 m)	
Binding	⅝ yd. (.6 m)	
Backing	3¼ yds. (3 m)	
Batting (packaged)	72" x 90" (180 cm x 225 cm)	
Batting (45" wide)	3⅛ yds. (2.9 m)	

Cutting (Refer to *Cutting For Machine Piecing*, page 25):
59 whole blocks, 20 half blocks, 4 quarter blocks

Muslin	256 - Template A
	24 - Template C
	24 - Template C reversed
Pastels	280 - Template B
	280 - Template B reversed
Border	6 crossgrain cuts 4½" wide
Binding	6 crossgrain cuts 2½" wide

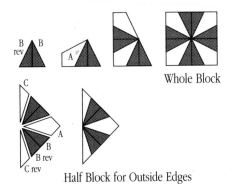

Whole Block

Half Block for Outside Edges

Quarter Block for Corners

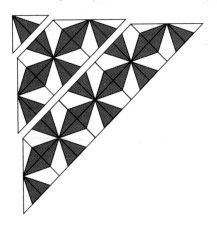

Directions:

Use ¼" seam allowances throughout. Refer to *Quiltmaking Techniques*, page 25, for specific sewing methods. Refer to quilt diagram, color photo and piecing diagrams for order of assembling. Refer to page 18 for personalization techniques.

1. Whole block: Sew B and B reversed together. Make 4. Add A to left side of each as shown. Sew 2 units together to make 2 halves: sew 2 halves together to make whole block. Make 59. Press.

2. Half block: Sew 2 Bs together 2 times. Sew 1 A between B units as shown. Sew 2 Cs to other sides of Bs. Make 20. Press.

3. Quarter blocks: Sew 2 Bs together; sew C to each side as shown. Make 4. Press.

4. Sew blocks, half blocks, and quarter blocks into diagonal rows following diagram.

5. Sew rows together.

6. For mitered border, follow cutting directions above and refer to *Mitered Borders* section of *Quiltmaking Techniques*, page 90, for joining it to the quilt.

7. Refer to *Finishing Steps For All Quilts*, page 51. Quilt is hand quilted ¼" from seams, and a star pattern is quilted in the border (pattern on page 100).

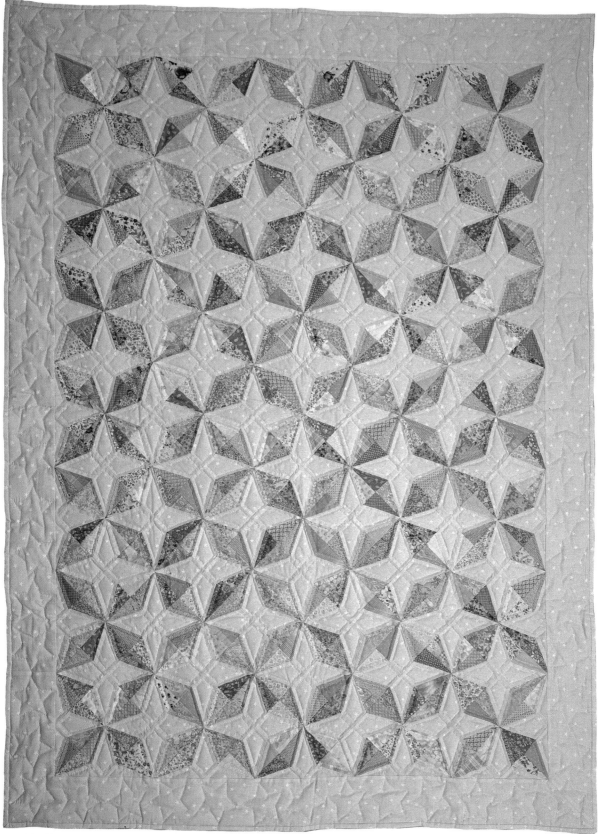

GENTLE TIMES. Designed by Nancy Smith and Lynda Milligan; hand quilted by Gwenn Michal; 1991; Denver, Colorado; 50″ x 67″. Inspired by an antique quilt, this pattern leaves room for the imagination. Any number of color combinations could be used. We have intentionally left it unpersonalized to show that not all memory quilts *have* to be personalized. It could, however, very easily be a signature quilt. Even though there are twelve points meeting in the center of each block, it sews together very nicely.

Other suggested uses: Use the block for a friendship exchange. Specify the color scheme or let the scraps used by the participants set the color scheme. The stars in the border would be fun places to autograph.

HOMESPUN MEMORIES

APPROXIMATE FINISHED SIZE 50″ x 58″
8″ BLOCK - 30 blocks set 5 x 6
SETTING - Blocks set straight
TECHNIQUE - Patchwork with permanent marking pen.

Yardage (42″- 45″ or 107-114 cm wide):
Blocks

Muslin	⅓ yd. (.3 m)
Star fabrics to total	1½ yds. (1.4 m)
Backgrounds to total	1⅝ yds. (1.5 m)
Border	1⅛ yds. (1.1 m)
Binding	⅝ yd. (.6 m)
Backing	3¼ yds. (3 m)
Batting (packaged)	72″ x 90″ (180 cm x 225 cm)
Batting (45″ wide)	3 yds. (2.8 m)

Cutting (Refer to *Cutting For Machine Piecing*, page 25):

Muslin	30 - Template A
Star fabrics	60 - Template A
	240 - Template C
Backgrounds	120 - Template B (2½″ x 2½″)
	240 - Template C
Border	6 crossgrain cuts 5½″ wide
Binding	6 crossgrain cuts 2½″ wide

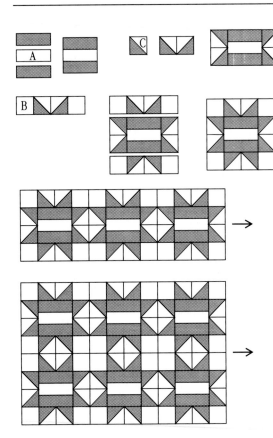

Directions:

Use ¼″ seam allowances throughout. Refer to *Quiltmaking Techniques*, page 25, for specific sewing methods. Refer to quilt diagram, color photo and piecing diagrams for order of assembling. Refer to page 18 for personalization techniques.

1. Sew autograph center of star by sewing 3 A strips together. See diagram. Press seams toward dark fabric.
2. Sew remainder of block following diagram. Make 30 blocks. Press.
3. Sew 6 horizontal rows of 5 blocks.
4. Sew rows together.
5. For border, follow cutting directions above and refer to *Stairstep Borders* section of *Quiltmaking Techniques*, page 90. Sew border to top and bottom of quilt first, then sides.
6. Refer to *Finishing Steps For All Quilts*, page 51. Quilt is machine quilted from edge to edge in vertical and horizontal lines which follow seams in blocks.

HOMESPUN MEMORIES. Designed by Nancy Smith and Lynda Milligan; machine quilted by Sharon Holmes; 1991; Denver, Colorado; 50″ x 58″. Signature strips adorn this homespun variation of the Variable Star quilt block. A soft and usable remembrance filled with personal statements, this quilt would keep any cold body warm! Although the quilt has only signatures, the space is large enough for short messages or special thoughts. The homespun fabric, being soft and mellow, adds to the symbolism of the quilt as an everlasting celebration of friendship.

Other suggested uses: This design works well for a block exchange among friends or a signature block that could be sent out already pieced to friends for embellishment.

IT'S MY NEIGHBORHOOD

APPROXIMATE FINISHED SIZE 35″ x 41″
5¼″ HOUSE BLOCK - 2⅝″ x 5¼″ TREE BLOCK
15 house blocks and 20 tree blocks set alternately
SETTING - House blocks set alternately with tree blocks and separated by horizontal sashing of sky fabric.
TECHNIQUE - Patchwork with fine permanent marking pen.

Yardage (42″- 45″ or 107-114 cm wide):

Sky (includes sashing)	1 yd. (1 m)
Roofs - reds to total	⅙ yd. (.2 m)
Houses, chimneys, tree trunks - blues & browns to total	½ yd. (.5 m)
Windows, doors - creams to total	⅛ yd. (.2 m)
Grass, trees - green prints to total	⅝ yd. (.6 m)
Grass (house block) - green solid	¼ yd. (.3 m)
Border 1	¼ yd. (.3 m)
Border 2	¼ yd. (.3 m)
Border 3	½ yd. (.5 m)
Binding	⅜ yd. (.4 m)
Backing	1⅓ yds. (1.3 m)
Batting (packaged)	45″ x 60″ (112.5 cm x 150 cm)
Batting (45″ wide)	1⅓ yds. (1.3 m)

Cutting (Refer to *Cutting For Machine Piecing*, page 25):

Sky	20 - Template I
	20 - Template I reversed
	70 - Template C
	30 - Template D
	30 - Template G
	15 - Template B
	5 crossgrain cuts 1¾″ wide
Roofs	15 - Template F
Houses	60 - Template B
	15 - Template C
	15 - Template E
Chimneys	30 - Template C
Tree trunks	20 - Template C
Windows	15 - Template C
Doors	15 - Template B
Grass (prints)	20 - Template J
Grass (solid)	15 - Template A
Trees	20 - Template H
Border 1	4 crossgrain cuts 1½″ wide
Border 2	4 crossgrain cuts 1″ wide
Border 3	4 crossgrain cuts 3½″ wide
Binding	4 crossgrain cuts 2½″ wide

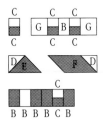

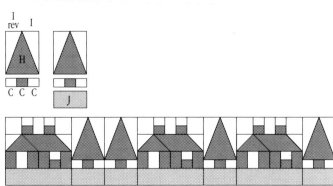

Directions:

Use ¼″ seam allowances throughout. Refer to *Quiltmaking Techniques*, page 25, for specific sewing methods. Refer to quilt diagram, color photo and piecing diagrams for order of assembling. Refer to page 18 for personalization techniques.

1. House block: Construct block in 4 rows as shown, then join rows. See diagram for position of pieces. Make 15. Press.
2. Tree block: Construct block in 3 rows as shown, then join rows. See diagram for position of pieces. Make 20. Press.
3. Sew house and tree blocks into horizontal rows following whole quilt diagram. Not all rows are identical. Press.

(Continued on page 88)

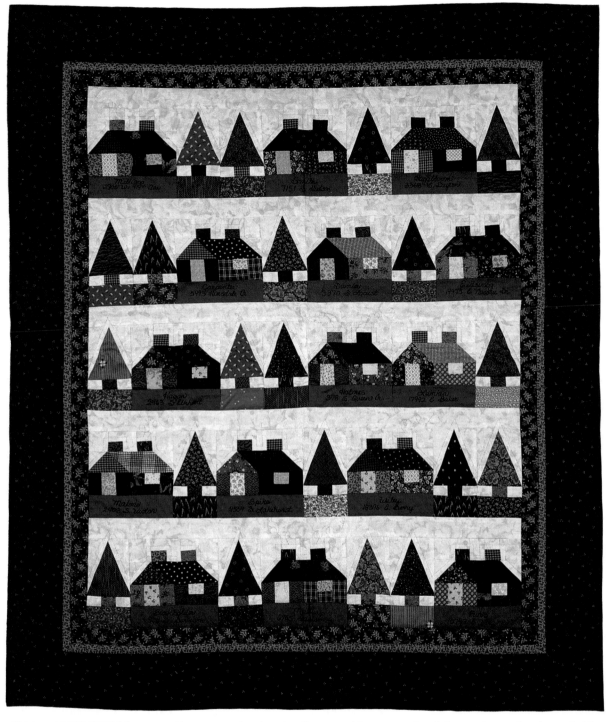

IT'S MY NEIGHBORHOOD. Designed by Nancy Smith and Lynda Milligan; pieced by Nancy Smith and Sharon Holmes, and machine quilted by Sharon; 1991; Denver, Colorado; 35″ x 41″. Many of us get so attached to our neighborhoods and friends that if we have to move, it is very traumatic. We designed this quilt to help keep the old ties. This quilt can be made any size; the only thing to remember in your planning is that two tree blocks equal one house block.

Other suggested uses: Send the pattern to your friends and have them make the houses in colors that are similar to their own real homes. The doors and windows can also be decorated and embellished with wreaths, curtains, or faces. What fun to think of the possibilities!

MEMORY QUILT

APPROXIMATE FINISHED SIZE 84″ x 72″
10″ BLOCKS - 30 blocks set 6 x 5
SETTING - Blocks set straight with pieced sashing and setting squares that form stars.
TECHNIQUE - Patchwork and hand embroidery.

Yardage (42″- 45″ or 107-114 cm wide):
Blocks
Muslin	1⅞ yds. (1.8 m)
Yellow solids to total	¾ yd. (.7 m)
Yellow prints to total	1¼ yds. (1.2 m)

Sashing
Muslin	1⅝ yds. (1.5 m)
Yellow solid	⅝ yd. (.6 m)
Borders 1, 2, 3	⅔ yd. each (.6 m)
Binding	⅔ yd. (.6 m)
Backing	4½ yds. (4.2 m)
Batting (packaged)	81″ x 96″ (202.5 cm x 240 cm)
Batting (45″ wide)	4⅜ yds. (4 m)

Cutting (Refer to *Cutting For Machine Piecing*, page 25):
Muslin	30 - Template A (2½″ x 6½″)
	60 - Template B (2½″ x 2½″)
	120 - Template D
	49 - Template E (3″ x 10½″)
	20 - Template C (3″ x 3″)
Yellow solids (blocks)	120 - Template B (2½″ x 2½″)
Yellow Prints	120 - Template D
Yellow solid (sashing stars)	196 - Template F (1¾″ x 1¾″)
Border 1	8 crossgrain cuts 2½″ wide
Border 2	8 crossgrain cuts 2½″ wide
Border 3	8 crossgrain cuts 2½″ wide
Binding	8 crossgrain cuts 2½″ wide

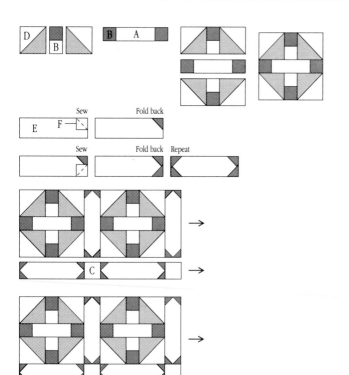

Directions:

Use ¼″ seam allowances throughout. Refer to *Quiltmaking Techniques*, page 25, for specific sewing methods. Refer to quilt diagram, color photo and piecing diagrams for order of assembling. Refer to page 18 for personalization techniques.

1. Construct block in 3 rows as shown, then join rows. Make 30. Press.
2. Piece 49 sashing strips: Place F on one corner of E, right sides together and raw edges even. Sew diagonally as shown. Fold back to form triangle. Repeat for other 3 corners. Press.
3. Sew 5 horizontal rows alternating 6 blocks and 5 sashing strips. Sew 4 horizontal sashing rows alternating 6 sashing strips and 5 piece C.
4. Sew alternating rows of blocks and sashing together following diagram.
5. For borders, follow cutting directions above and refer to *Stairstep Borders* section of *Quiltmaking Techniques*, page 90. Sew borders to top and bottom first, then sides.
6. Refer to *Finishing Steps For All Quilts*, page 51. Quilt is hand quilted in a combination of outline quilting, crosses, and cables (cable patterns on page 100).

MEMORY QUILT. Designed and made by the friends of Maggie Price; 1937; Aurora, Colorado; 84″ x 72″. This quilt is owned by Maggie's great niece, Melva Hahn. Melva remembers some of the stories her aunt told about the ladies whose names appear on this beautiful quilt. She also enjoys it because it was made in the same year her husband was born. The quilt is unusual because of the number of yellow prints and solids. The blocks are set together with muslin corners and strips. The tiny yellow triangles on the corners of the strips form the little stars when set with the sashing squares.

Other suggested uses: This quilt has room for many more signatures and special messages. The sashing strips as well as the centers of the little stars can be used for signatures. The small sashing squares that make up the little stars would be a terrific place for photo transfers.

PINWHEELS AND CRAYONS

APPROXIMATE FINISHED SIZE 43″x 43″
12″ BLOCK - 9 blocks set 3 x 3
SETTING - Blocks set straight.
TECHNIQUE - Patchwork with permanent marking pen.

Yardage (42"- 45" or 107-114 cm wide):
Blocks
Muslin	1 yd. (1 m)
Black solid	1⅛ yds. (1.1 m)
Prints	⅙ yd. each of 5 prints (.2 m)
Border 1 (black solid)	¼ yd. (.3 m)
Borders 2, 3	¼ yd.each of 4 prints (.3 m)
Binding	½ yd. (.5 m)
Backing	1⅜ yds. or 2¾ yds. depending on shrinkage (1.3 m or 2.6 m)
Batting (packaged)	45″ x 60″ (112.5 cm x 150 cm)
Batting (45″ wide)	1⅓ yds. (1.3 m)
Embroidery floss	1-2 skeins

Cutting (Refer to *Cutting For Machine Piecing*, page 25):
Choose Traditional *or* Strip Piecing Method.
Traditional Method
Muslin	9 - Template A (9″ x 9″)
Black	36 - Template C
Prints	36 - Template B
Border 1	5 crossgrain cuts 1¼″ wide
Borders 2, 3	3 crossgrain cuts 2″ wide from each of 4 prints
Binding	5 crossgrain cuts 2½″ wide

Strip Piecing Method
Muslin	9 - pieces 9″ x 9″
Black	10 crossgrain cuts 3½″ wide
Prints	5 crossgrain cuts 3¾″ wide
Borders	as above
Binding	as above

Traditional Method

Strip Piecing Method

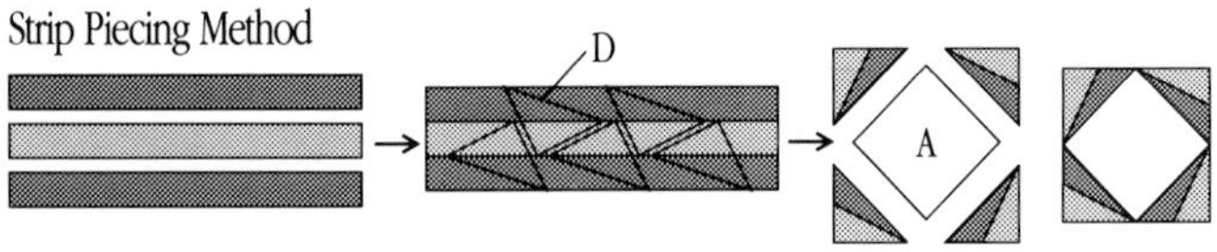

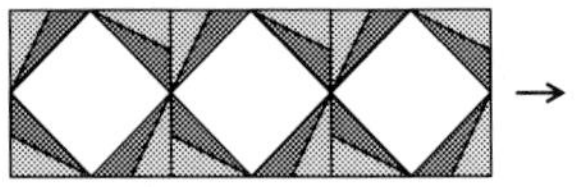

Directions:

Use ¼″ seam allowances throughout. Refer to *Quiltmaking Techniques*, page 25, for specific sewing methods. Refer to quilt diagram, color photo and piecing diagrams for order of assembling. Refer to page 20 for coloring techniques.

1. Color 9″ blocks.
2. Traditional Method: Sew B to C 36 times. Sew B/C units to A. Make 9 blocks. Press seams toward outside edges of blocks.
3. Strip Piecing Method: Make 5 black-print-black strip sets. Press seams toward center strip. Make template D of plastic; transfer gray line to plastic. Lay plastic template on right side of strip set matching gray line on template to seamline on strip set as shown. Draw around template. Slide template to next position shown (keep same side up for marking all pieces), and draw around it again. Continue to end of strip; cut out. Sew D units to A. Make 9 blocks. Press seams toward outside edges of blocks.
4. Sew blocks together into 3 horizontal rows of 3 blocks each.
5. Sew rows together.
6. For mitered borders, follow cutting directions above and refer to *Mitered Borders* section of *Quiltmaking Techniques*, page 90. Refer to color photo for color placement of borders.
7. Press quilt top well. Piece backing to 47″ square. Layer 47″ square of batting, then quilt backing right side up, then quilt top right side down. Pin edges well. Sew around all 4 sides leaving an opening on one side to turn. Trim backing and batting to same size as quilt top. Trim corners; turn; press lightly. Slipstitch opening closed. Referring to page 92, tie quilt with embroidery floss at corners of blocks and at corners of illustrated sections of blocks.

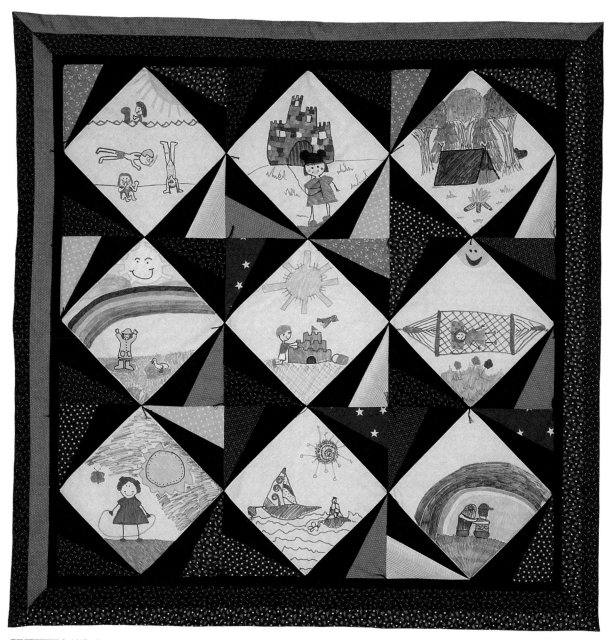

PINWHEELS AND CRAYONS. Designed by Nancy Smith and Lynda Milligan; pictures by Emily, Anna, and Shea Robinson; tied by Sharon Holmes; 1991; Denver, Colorado; 43″ x 43″. We liked the little block of "Dear Amelia" so well that we decided to enlarge it for use with other techniques. Marilyn Robinson's children drew several pictures on paper. We drew guidelines of the squares to begin with because the blocks are placed on point. We asked them to fill the square as much as possible. They chose their favorite designs and transferred the outlines to the fabric squares with the use of a light box. They then colored in the designs with fabric markers. We wanted to complement the designs with the fabric, so we chose the bright crayon colors set with black for the pinwheels. To make the border more interesting, we rotated the colors.

Other suggested uses: This larger block would lend itself very well to the use of collages of photo transfers; applique or stenciling would fill the blocks also.

PHOTO ALBUM

APPROXIMATE FINISHED SIZE 41″ x 41″
6″ BLOCK - 16 blocks set 4 x 4
SETTING - Blocks set straight with framing and sashing.
TECHNIQUE - Patchwork and photo transfers.

Yardage (42″- 45″ or 107-114 cm wide):
Blocks
Muslin	¾ yd. (.7 m)	
Black (corners)	¼ yd. (.3 m)	

Frames
Beige solid	1 yd. (1 m)	

Sashing
Black solid	⅝ yd. (.6 m)	
Binding	⅜ yd. (.4 m)	
Backing	1⅓ yds. (1.3 m)	
Batting (packaged)	45″ x 60″ (112.5 cm x 150 cm)	
Batting (45″ wide)	1¼ yds. (1.2 m)	

Cutting (Refer to *Cutting For Machine Piecing*, page 25):
Muslin	16 - Template A (6½″ x 6½″)
Beige	32 - Template B (2″ x 6½″)
	32 - Template C (2″ x 9½″)
Black	64 - Template D (1½″ x 1½″)
	10 crossgrain cuts 1½″ wide
Binding	4 crossgrain cuts 2½″ wide

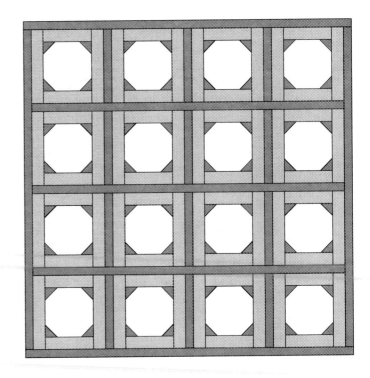

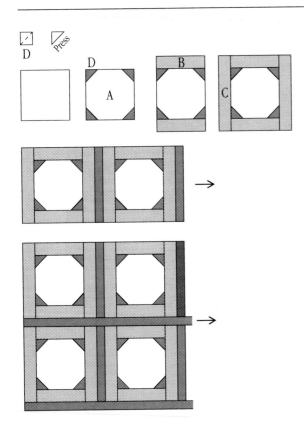

Directions:

Use ¼″ seam allowances throughout. Refer to *Quiltmaking Techniques*, page 25, for specific sewing methods. Refer to quilt diagram, color photo and piecing diagrams for order of assembling. Refer to page 23 for photo transfer techniques.

1. Transfer laser copy photos onto 6½″ squares.
2. Fold piece D in half diagonally and press. Place on one corner of A with raw edges even and stitch in place along raw edges. Repeat for other 3 corners of A. Make 16 blocks. See diagram.
3. Add B to top and bottom of A.
4. Add C to sides of A. Press blocks.
5. Cut 1½″ wide black strips into 12 sashing strips 9½″ long. Sew 4 rows alternating 4 blocks and 3 black sashing strips. See diagram.
6. Cut 1½″ wide black strips into 3 sashing strips 39½″ long. Sew alternating rows of blocks and sashing together following diagram..
7. For border, sew remaining 4 black strips to quilt top referring to *Stairstep Borders* Section of *Quiltmaking Techniques*, page 90. Sew borders to sides first, then top and bottom.
8. Refer to *Finishing Steps For All Quilts*, page 51. Quilt is hand quilted around photos and down centers of beige solid strips.

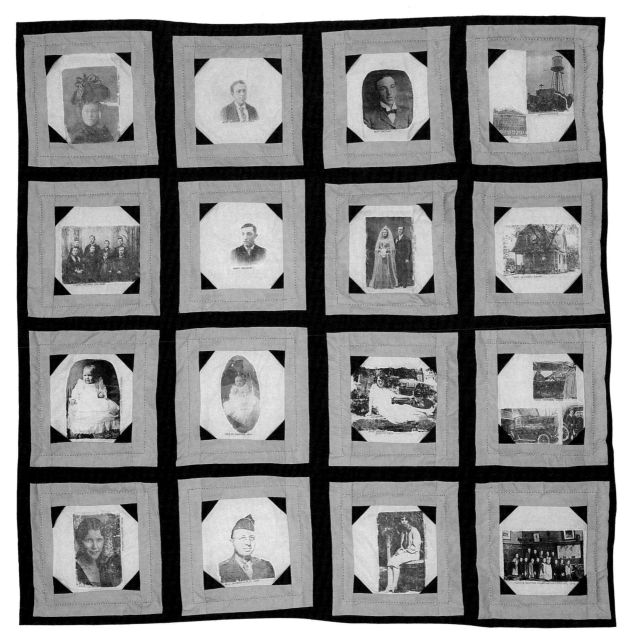

PHOTO ALBUM. Designed and made by Mary Christofferson; 1991; Littleton, Colorado; 41″ x 41″. During our lifetimes, we have all let our hearts wander through photo albums. Mary has moved out of the paper pages found in traditional albums and created her own unique remembrance album in fabric. Mary became more familiar with her ancestors as she worked with their photos and their geneology, and she was particularly delighted that her children and grandchildren became more acquainted with their family history. Mary experimented with many of the transfer solutions on the market and finally came up with her own. Note that the black corners that "hold" the photographs are loose to represent the real thing. This photo shows only a portion of the original quilt.

Other suggested uses: The 6″ blocks can be used for applique or stenciling. Children's artwork can be reduced or enlarged to fit these squares and made into photo transfers. What a wonderful portfolio that would make!

RACHEL'S QUILT

APPROXIMATE FINISHED SIZE 48″ x 57″
6″ BLOCK - 30 blocks set 5 x 6
SETTING - Blocks set straight with strip-pieced sashing and nine-patch setting squares.
TECHNIQUE - Patchwork and photo transfers made by laser color copier.

Yardage (42″- 45″ or 107-114 cm wide):
Blocks
    Muslin   1⅛ yds. (1.1 m)
Sashing
    Muslin   1⅛ yds. (1.1 m)
    Pastels to total   1⅝ yds. (1.5 m)
Binding   ⅝ yd. (.6 m)
Backing   3 yds. (2.8 m)
Batting (packaged) 72″ x 90″ (180 cm x 225 cm)
Batting (45″ wide) 3 yds. (2.8 m)

Cutting (Refer to *Cutting For Machine Piecing*, page 25):
Choose Traditional *or* Strip Piecing Method.
Traditional Method
    Muslin   30 - Template A (6½″ x 6½″)
               71 - Template C (1½″ x 6½″)
              210 - Template B (1½″ x 1½″)
    Pastels   142 - Template C (1½″ x 6½″)
              168 - Template B (1½″ x 1½″)
    Binding   6 crossgrain cuts 2½″ wide
Strip Piecing Method
    Muslin   22 crossgrain cuts 1½″ wide
    Pastels   32 crossgrain cuts 1½″ wide
    Binding   as above

Traditional Method

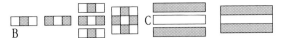
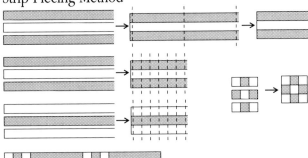

Strip Piecing Method

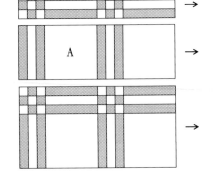

Directions:

Use ¼″ seam allowances throughout. Refer to *Quiltmaking Techniques*, page 25, for specific sewing methods. Refer to quilt diagram, color photo and piecing diagrams for order of assembling. Refer to page 23 for photo transfer techniques.

1. Transfer laser copy photos onto 6½″ blocks.
2. Traditional Method: Piece 42 9-patch setting squares following diagram. Piece 71 sashing strips together following diagram. Press seams toward pastels.
3. Strip Piecing Method: *For setting squares*, make 2 pastel-muslin-pastel strip sets, press seams, and cut 42 segments 1½″ wide. *Also for setting squares*, make 4 muslin-pastel-muslin strip sets, press seams toward pastels, and cut them into 84 segments 1½″ wide. Assemble and sew into blocks following diagram. *For sashing strips*, make 12 pastel-muslin-pastel strip sets, press seams toward pastels, and cut them into 71 segments 6½″ wide (see diagram).
4. Sew 7 horizontal sashing rows alternating 6 setting squares and 5 sashing strips following diagram. Sew 6 horizontal rows alternating 6 sashing strips and 5 piece A.
5. Sew alternating rows of blocks and sashing together following diagram.
6. Refer to *Finishing Steps For All Quilts*, page 51. Quilt is machine quilted in the ditch.

RACHEL'S QUILT. Designed by Nancy Smith for Rachel Smith to celebrate her high school graduation; machine quilted by Sharon Holmes; 1990; Denver, Colorado; 48″ x 57″. Nancy's daughter grew up with two friends from the time they were in first grade. Nancy collected the photos from over the years and made them into photo transfers. She set the quilt together with muslin strips surrounded by scrap strips for a triple sashing. This set off each photo very nicely. Nancy also made a quilt for each of the other girls and presented them at their graduation party.

Other suggested uses: The triple sashing border is very effective at setting off any type of block, and it adds another pattern as well as length and width. The blocks are 6″ and are very adaptable to any method of personalization.

READING... THE KEY TO IMAGINATION

APPROXIMATE FINISHED SIZE 48″ x 56″
8″ BLOCK - 30 blocks set 5 x 6
SETTING - Blocks set straight.
TECHNIQUE - Fabric paint and permanent markers.

Yardage (42″- 45″ or 107-114 m wide):
Blocks
     Muslin   2⅛ yds. (2 m)
Border   ⅞ yd. (.8 m)
Binding   ⅝ yd. (.6 m)
Backing   3 yds. (2.8 m)
Batting (packaged)   72″ x 90″ (180 cm x 225 cm)
Batting (45″ wide)   3 yds. (2.8 m)

Cutting (Refer to *Cutting For Machine Piecing*, page 25):
Muslin   30 - Template A (8½″ x 8½″)
Border   5 crossgrain cuts 4½″ wide
Binding   6 crossgrain cuts 2½″ wide

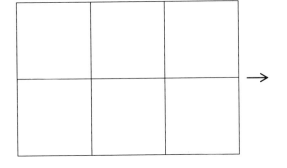

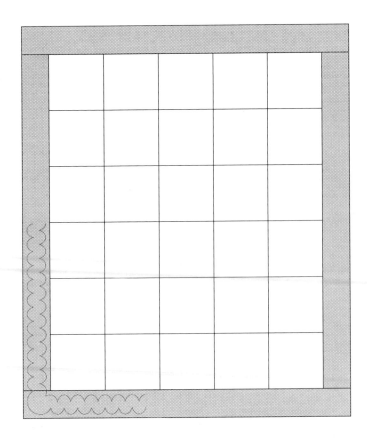

Directions:

Use ¼″ seam allowances throughout. Refer to *Quiltmaking Techniques*, page 25, for specific sewing methods. Refer to quilt diagram, color photo and piecing diagrams for order of assembling. Refer to page 20 for hints on drawing and coloring on fabric.

1. Paint and personalize 8½″ blocks.
2. Sew 6 horizontal rows of 5 blocks each following diagram.
3. Sew rows together.
4. For border, follow cutting directions above and refer to *Stairstep Borders* section of *Quiltmaking Techniques*, page 90.
5. Refer to *Finishing Steps For All Quilts*, page 51. Quilt is hand quilted around shapes in blocks, and a rope design is quilted in the border (pattern on page 100).

READING...THE KEY TO IMAGINATION. Blocks made by second graders at Vivian Elementary School in Jefferson County, Colorado; assembled and finished by Adrianne Stauffer; 1990; Lakewood, Colorado; 48″ x 56″. Adrianne (Andy) intended to expose her class to the love of books while they learned about the art form of quilting. As she read the stories of Tomie dePaola, the children did drawings and tracings on paper to represent their favorites. With help from Andy, they transferred these drawings onto fabric and colored them in with Faber Castell markers. Andy did the writing on the blocks according to the children's wishes. Not only did the children share their love of reading and Tomie dePaola's stories, but they created a beautiful quilt.

Other suggested uses: The 8″ blocks in this quilt can be personalized in any way. The space is large enough for an applique or for a collage of photo transfers.

SIX-POINTED STAR MEMORY QUILT

APPROXIMATE FINISHED SIZE 43″ x 52″
8¾″ DIAMETER UNIT - 32 whole units and 6 half units set 5 x 7
SETTING - Units and half-units set with hexagons.
TECHNIQUE - Patchwork with hand embroidery.

Yardage (42″- 45″ or 107-144 cm wide):
Star units
Solids to total	⅜ yd. (.4 m)	
Prints to total	2¼ yds. (2.1 m)	
	(⅛ yd. or .2 m each of 38 prints)	
Setting hexagons (muslin)	2 yds. (1.9 m)	
Binding	½ yd. (.5 m)	
Backing	1⅝ yds. or 2¾ yds. depending on shrinkage	
	(1.5 m or 2.6 m)	
Batting (packaged)	45″ x 60″ (112.5 cm x 150 cm)	
Batting (45″ wide)	1⅜ yds. (1.3 m)	

Cutting (Refer to *Cutting For Machine Piecing*, page 25):
Solids	38 - Template B
Prints	210 - Template A
Muslin	88 - Template C
Binding	5 crossgrain cuts 2½″ wide

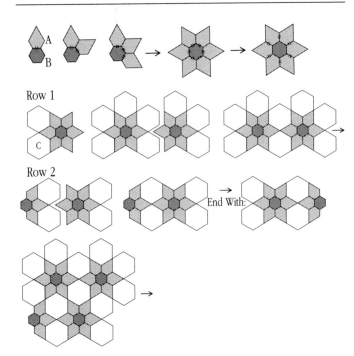

Directions:

Use ¼″ seam allowances throughout. Refer to *Quiltmaking Techniques*, page 25, for specific sewing methods. Refer to quilt diagram, color photo and piecing diagrams for order of assembling. Refer to page 20 for embroidery techniques.

1. Whole units: Sew 6 A (star points) to 1 B (center), then sew A to A around the unit as shown. *Leave seam allowances free by sewing to seam intersections rather than to cut edges.* Backstitch at seam intersections. Make 32.

2. Half units: Follow step 1 but add 3 A to each B. Make 6.

3. Sew into horizontal rows by adding C around star units as shown. Note that odd rows begin with whole blocks, and even rows begin with half blocks. Leave seam allowances free and backstitch as before.

4. Sew alternating rows together leaving seam·allowances free; backstitch as before.

5. Press quilt top. Trim away hexagons at outer edge of quilt ¼″ from star points as shown. Outer line is cutting line; inner line is seamline.

6. Embroider names if not already done.

7. Refer to *Finishing Steps For All Quilts*, page 51. Quilt is outline quilted by hand.

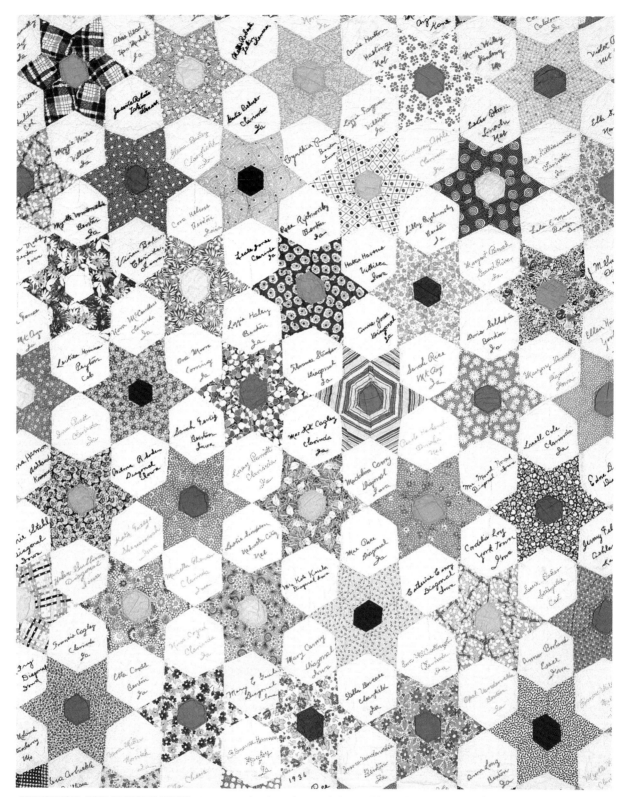

SIX-POINTED STAR MEMORY QUILT. Designer and maker unknown; quilt owned by Linda Nolte Evans; 1936; Greenwood Village, Colorado; 43″ x 52″. This quilt was probably made in Iowa. It features six-pointed stars made of prints, stripes, and checks of the 1930s. Muslin hexagons join the stars, and each is embroidered with a name, city, and state (mainly Iowa, Nebraska, Kansas, and Colorado). This is a wonderful example of a scrap autograph quilt. This photo shows only a portion of the original quilt.

Other suggested uses: This is another great pattern to send to your friends. Quiltmaking friends could make the blocks from their own scraps and sign the muslin hexagons, and non-quilters could be asked simply to sign the muslin hexagons.

STARS AND STRIPES FOREVER

APPROXIMATE FINISHED SIZE 39″ x 52″
4″ BLOCK - 48 blocks set 6 x 8
SETTING - Blocks set straight with pieced sashing and setting squares that form stars.
TECHNIQUE - Patchwork with permanent marking pen.

Yardage (42″- 45″ or 107-114 cm wide):

Blocks
Muslin	⅞ yd. (.8 m)

Sashing
Muslin	½ yd. (.5 m)
Red solid	1 yd. (1 m)
Blue print	1 yd. (1 m)

Border
Muslin	¼ yd. (.3 m)
Red solid	½ yd. (.5 m)
Binding	½ yd. (.5 m)
Backing	1⅝ yds. (1.5 m)
Batting (packaged)	45″ x 60″ (112.5 cm x 150 cm)
Batting (45″ wide)	1⅝ yds. (1.5 m)

Cutting (Refer to *Cutting For Machine Piecing*, page 25):
Choose Traditional *or* Strip Piecing Method.

Traditional Method
Muslin	48 - Template A (4½″ x 4½″)
	82 - Template C (1¼″ x 4½″)
Red solid	164 - Template C (1¼″ x 4½″)
Blue print	35 - Template B (2¾″ x 2¾″)
	280 - Template D (1⅝″ x 1⅝″)
Border 1	5 crossgrain cuts 1¼″ wide
Border 2	5 crossgrain cuts 1¼″ wide
Border 3	5 crossgrain cuts 1¼″ wide
Binding	5 crossgrain cuts 2½″ wide

Strip Piecing Method
Muslin	48 - pieces 4½″ x 4½″
	11 crossgrain cuts 1¼″ wide
Red solid	22 crossgrain cuts 1¼″ wide
Blue print	35 - pieces 2¾″ x 2¾″
	280 - pieces 1⅝″ x 1⅝″
Borders	as above
Binding	as above

Traditional Method

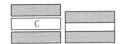

Strip Piecing Method

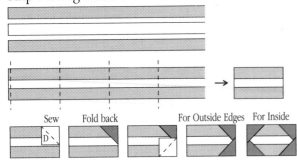

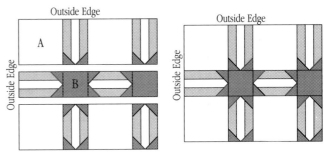

Directions:

Use ¼″ seam allowances throughout. Refer to *Quiltmaking Techniques*, page 25, for specific sewing methods. Refer to quilt diagram, color photo and piecing diagrams for order of assembling. Refer to page 18 for personalization techniques.

1. Traditional Method: Make 82 sashing strips by sewing 3 Cs together as shown. Press seams toward red fabric.
2. Strip Piecing Method: Make 11 red-muslin-red strip sets, press seams toward red, and cut them into 4½″ segments. See diagram.

(Continued on page 88)

STARS AND STRIPES FOREVER. Designed by Nancy Smith and Lynda Milligan; calligraphy by Linda Gutin; machine quilted by Sharon Holmes; 1991; Denver, Colorado; 39″ x 52″. Open spaces such as those found in this quilt create opportunities for commemorating special events or expressing shared feelings. This patriotic quilt includes some of the quotations that exemplify the strength and courage of our ancestors and have helped form our image of ourselves as a nation. The stripes and the stars are actually the sashing strips that set the squares together.

Other suggested uses: Because the actual autograph pieces are just 4″ squares, they can easily be precut and sent out to participants. In the meantime, the sashing strips can be assembled. Picture this quilt with stars in bright crayon colors surrounding children's drawings, perhaps self-portraits. Children could also add their favorite saying. Another idea would be to use photo transfers for the squares and make the quilt represent the stars of someone's life. See other color combinations on page 34.

THANKS FOR THE MEMORIES

APPROXIMATE FINISHED SIZE 56" x 70"
12" BLOCK - 12 blocks set 3 x 4
SETTING - Blocks set straight with sashing and setting squares.
TECHNIQUE - Patchwork and photo transfers made by laser color copier.

Yardage (42"- 45" or 107-114 cm wide):
Blocks
    Muslin   1⅝ yds. (1.5 m)
    Green print   ⅔ yd. (.6 m)
Sashing (includes Border 1)
    Print   1½ yds. (1.4 m)
Border 2   ½ yd. (.5 m)
Border 3   ¾ yd. (.7 m)
Binding   ⅝ yd. (.6 m)
Backing   3½ yds. (3.2 m)
Batting (packaged)   72" x 90" (180 cm x 225 cm)
Batting (45" wide)   3⅜ yds. (3.1 m)

Cutting (Refer to *Cutting For Machine Piecing*, page 25):
Muslin   12 - Template A (12½" x 12½")
Green print   6 - Template C (3" x 3")
                 48 - Template D (3½" x 3½")
Sashing print 17 - Template B (3" x 12½")
Border 1   7 crossgrain cuts 4" wide
Border 2   7 crossgrain cuts 2" wide
Border 3   7 crossgrain cuts 3" wide
Binding   7 crossgrain cuts 2½" wide

Sew   Fold Back

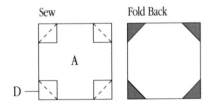

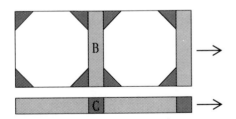

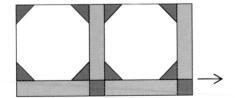

Directions:

Use ¼" seam allowances throughout. Refer to *Quiltmaking Techniques*, page 25, for specific sewing methods. Refer to quilt diagram, color photo and piecing diagrams for order of assembling. Refer to page 23 for photo transfer techniques.

1. Transfer laser copy photos onto 12½" squares.
2. Make 12 blocks: Place D on one corner of A, right sides together and raw edges even. Sew diagonally as shown. Fold back to form triangle. Repeat for other 3 corners. Press. If desired to reduce bulk, lift D and cut away triangular section of D (lower part only) and A leaving ¼" seam allowance.
3. Sew 4 horizontal block rows alternating 3 blocks and 2 piece B. Sew 3 horizontal sashing rows alternating 3 piece B and 2 piece C.
4. Sew alternating rows of blocks and sashing together following diagram.
5. For mitered borders, follow cutting directions above and refer to *Mitered Borders* section of *Quiltmaking Techniques*, page 90, for joining them to the quilt.
6. Refer to *Finishing Steps For All Quilts*, page 51. Quilt is machine quilted around photos and in the ditch between blocks, sashing and borders.

THANKS FOR THE MEMORIES. Designed and made by Judy Carpenter for her mother, Lola Kirsch, in celebration of her 75th birthday; 1990; Fort Wayne, Indiana; 56″ x 70″. What better way to remember and honor a special person in your life? Judy grouped pictures into collages representing different aspects of her mother's life. In the upper right hand corner, she transferred pictures of the three houses that her parents lived in during their married life. Another block shows Judy's sister and family. Another has pictures of all her grandchildren from birth to the present, and yet another shows Judy and her sister growing up. One special block chronicles the events of her parents' married life. This quilt is a wonderful memory of times shared with loved ones.

Other suggested uses: The 12″ block is large enough for a number of uses. A friendship block exchange, children's artwork, and applique are just some of the choices.

THREADS OF TIME

APPROXIMATE FINISHED SIZE 33" x 37"
4" BLOCK - 42 blocks set 6 x 7
SETTING - Blocks set straight but in alternating directions.
TECHNIQUE - Patchwork and fine permanent marking pen.

Yardage (42"- 45" or 107-114 cm wide):
Blocks
    Muslin   ⅝ yd. (.6 m)
    Stripes   42 scraps at least 3" x 3" (or prints to total ¼ yd.) (.3 m)
    Solids   42 scraps at least 4" x 6"(or ⅝ yd. total) (.6 m)
Border 1 (muslin)   ⅓ yd. (.3 m)
Border 2 (stripe)   1¼ yds. (1.2 m) (4 repeats needed)
Binding   ⅜ yd. (.4 m)
Backing   1⅛ yds. (1.1 m)
Batting (packaged) 45" x 60" (112.5 cm x 150 cm)
Batting (45" wide)   1 yd. (1 m)

Cutting (Refer to *Cutting For Machine Piecing*, page 25):
Muslin   84 - Template A
Stripes   42 - Template B (2½" x 2½")
Solids   84 - Template A
Border 1   4 crossgrain cuts 2" wide
Border 2   4 lengthwise cuts 3½" wide
Binding   4 crossgrain cuts 2½" wide

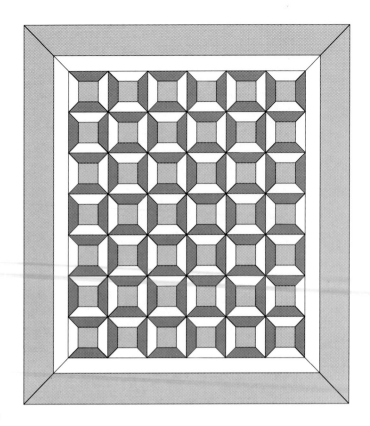

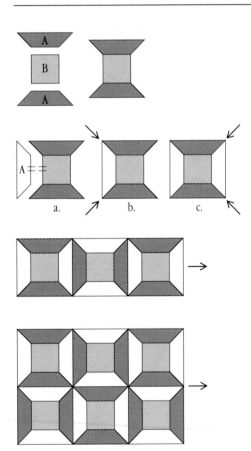

Directions:

Use ¼" seam allowances throughout. Refer to *Quiltmaking Techniques*, page 25, for specific sewing methods. Refer to quilt diagram, color photo and piecing diagrams for order of assembling. Refer to page 18 for personalization techniques.

1. Sew 2 A trapezoids (spool) to each B square (thread). *Leave seam allowance free at each corner by sewing to seam intersections rather than to cut edges.* Backstitch at seam intersections.

2. Sew 2 A trapezoids (background) to each spool in three steps:
   a. Sew seam between A and B.
   b. Sew one diagonal seam from outside *edge* of block toward inside (seam intersection). Sew other diagonal seam in same manner.
   c. Repeat for other side of block.

3. Press blocks.

4. Sew rows of blocks together alternating directions of blocks. Make 7 horizontal rows of 6 spools each.

5. Sew rows together.

6. For mitered borders, follow cutting directions above and refer to *Mitered Borders* section of *Quiltmaking Techniques*, page 90, for joining them to the quilt.

7. Refer to *Finishing Steps For All Quilts*, page 51. Quilt is machine quilted in the ditch between blocks, between borders, and between stripes in the wide outer border.

THREADS OF TIME. Designed by Nancy Smith and Lynda Milligan; stitched by Judy Carpenter and machine quilted by Sharon Holmes; 1991; Denver, Colorado; 33″ x 37″. A traditional and simple pattern, this is an excellent block for a group exchange as can be seen from all the spools quilts pictured in *The Gallery.* The threads from each of the spools are so symbolic of the ties that bind us together. The spaces in between the spools can be used for signatures or special sayings. The names can be simply written with a permanent marker, as we have done, or embroidered. Finding fabrics that represent wound thread is a pleasurable challenge. We have chosen to make the first border match the background fabric of the spools blocks. This allows a space for additional signatures or special sayings.

Other suggested uses: Looking at the black-and-white drawing of this quilt, you can see that the spools look like shadow boxes; by changing the coloring and using photo transfers for the "thread" squares, a very different look could be created.

BLUE FRIENDSHIP BLOCKS

(Continued from page 54)

vertical line on the ruler should line up point to point across the square. Using rotary cutter, trim off corners as shown. Repeat for other 3 sides of each block. Repeat the above for another round but begin by sewing 2¾″ x 4¾″ rectangles around the square.

3. Sew friendship squares together making 5 horizontal rows of 5 blocks each. Direction of signature triangles varies.
4. Sew rows together.
5. Embroider and personalize if not already done.
6. Refer to *Finishing Steps For All Quilts*, page 51. Quilt can be outline quilted around each concentric square.

GEMSTONES

(Continued from page 62)

3. Sew blocks together to form 10 horizontal rows of 8 blocks each.
4. Sew rows together.
5. For mitered border, follow cutting directions above and refer to *Mitered Borders* section of *Quiltmaking Techniques* page 90, for joining it to the quilt.
6. Embroider names on quilt if not already done.
7. Refer to *Finishing Steps For All Quilts*, page 51. Quilt is machine quilted from edge to edge in vertical and horizontal lines which follow seams between blocks.

IT'S MY NEIGHBORHOOD

(Continued from page 68)

4. Cut sky fabric sashing strips (1¾″ wide) into 5 pieces that measure the same length as patchwork rows (26¾″ if seam allowance is consistently ¼″). Sew a sashing strip to the top of each patchwork row; be careful not to stretch patchwork row.
5. Sew 5 rows together following diagram.
6. For borders, follow cutting directions above and refer to *Stairstep Borders* section of *Quiltmaking Techniques*, page 90. Sew borders to top and bottom first, then sides.
7. Refer to *Finishing Steps For All Quilts*, page 51.
8. Quilt is machine quilted ¼″ from roofs and tree tops, between rows of blocks and sashing, between borders, and in parallel lines the width of the sewing machine foot in the wide floral border.

STARS AND STRIPES FOREVER

(Continued from page 82)

3. Place D on one corner of a sashing strip, right sides together and raw edges even. Sew diagonally as shown. Fold back to form triangle. Repeat on opposite corner (see diagram). This makes one *outside* sashing strip. Make 23 more. Make 58 *inside* sashing strips with triangles on all 4 corners as shown. Press.
4. Sew block rows: Sew 2 horizontal rows alternating 6 piece A and 5 *outside* sashing strips (for top and bottom). Sew 6 horizontal rows alternating 6 piece A and 5 *inside* sashing strips.
5. Sew sashing rows: Sew 7 horizontal rows beginning and ending with *outside* sashing strips and alternating 5 piece B with 4 *inside* sashing strips. See diagram.
6. Sew alternating rows of blocks and sashing together following diagram.
7. For mitered borders, follow cutting directions above and refer to *Mitered Borders* section of *Quiltmaking Techniques*, page 90, for joining them to the quilt.
8. Refer to *Finishing Steps For All Quilts*, page 51. Quilt is machine quilted in the ditch between blocks and sashing.

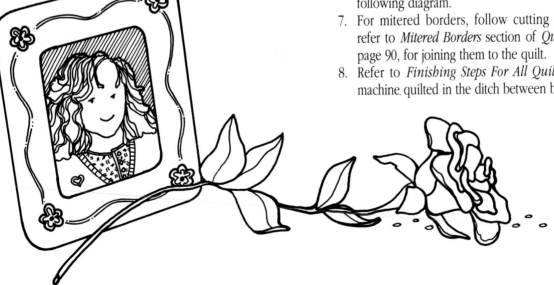

(Continued from page 26)

MACHINE APPLIQUE
Bondable Interfacing Method

1. Bond medium-weight, iron-on interfacing to back of applique fabric following manufacturer's directions. Cut appliques from bonded fabric. Do not include seam allowance. Use fabric glue stick sparingly to attach appliques to background fabric layering design from background to foreground.

2. Place a background stabilizer such as typing paper or Pellon® "Stitch N Tear"® under background fabric. Use a very short stitch length and a 1/16" to 1/8" wide zig-zag stitch width. Use a good quality thread. Loosen top tension as needed to keep bobbin thread from being visible on top of work. Keep the threads of the satin stitch at right angles to the edge of the applique by pivoting as needed. To pivot, leave needle in fabric, lift presser foot, turn fabric, lower foot, resume sewing. For outside curves, pivot when needle is on background fabric. For inside curves, pivot when needle is on applique fabric. To make tapered points, reduce stitch width while sewing. To tie off threads, bring stitch width to zero and take six to eight stitches next to the satin stitching. When finished sewing, tear away background stabilizer.

Fusing Web Method
(Pellon® "Wonder-Under"™ or Trans-Web™)

1. Trace patterns onto smooth, paper side of fusing web. *Trace patterns the reverse of the direction wanted.*

2. Press fusing web to wrong side of desired fabric with rough side facing fabric. Cut out shapes.

3. Peel off paper; position applique onto background fabric and press again; applique fuses to background. If design is layered, arrange all appliques before fusing.

4. For sewing, see step two under bondable interfacing method above.

HAND APPLIQUE

1. Make templates from patterns without adding seam allowances.

2. Place template down on *right* side of fabric and draw around it.

3. Cut pieces out by cutting 3/16" to 1/4" *outside* of drawn line.

4. Baste under all edges that are not overlapped by another piece by folding edges under on penciled line and basting in place with a single thread.
   a. Clip seam allowance on inside curves allowing fabric to spread.
   b. Clip inside angles up to seamline. When appliqueing these angles, take small overcast stitches to prevent fraying.

c. Miter outside points less than 90° in three separate folds: Fold down point; fold one edge to seamline; fold other edge to seamline. It may be necessary to trim corner before folding to reduce bulk.

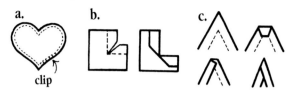

5. Pin or baste pieces to background fabric using pattern as a guide.

6. Applique with matching thread. Work stitches from right to left. Hide knot under applique or on back. To begin, bring needle up through applique and out the edge of the fold. Directly below where thread emerges from applique, take a tiny stitch through the background fabric bringing needle point immediately back up into the fold of the applique. Run the needle point along inside the fold for 1/8" to 1/4" and then out through the edge of the fold. Pull thread through. Repeat. Do not press applique pieces.

7. If the work is to be quilted, it is much easier and usually looks nicer if the backing fabric is removed from behind the larger applique pieces. Working from the wrong side with small, sharp scissors, carefully cut away the backing fabric up to 1/4" from the applique seamline. This also helps avoid the possibility of a darker background fabric showing through a lighter applique shape.

ASSEMBLING
Quilts Set Block to Block

1. Begin by laying out all the quilt blocks. Take a few minutes to stand back and view the arrangement. If using sparsely-patterned fabric, there may be an area of concentrated color that was not expected. By laying out all blocks, changes can be made before blocks are sewn together. Scrap quilt blocks often need some rearranging. A little bit of red or yellow in one of the fabrics may pop out, and distributing this color around the quilt may make a much more pleasing arrangement. This is a good time to decide if it would be preferable to separate the blocks with plain or pieced sashing strips and squares.

2. When the arrangement is pleasing, begin assembling. Sew all block units together into rows using a 1/4" seam allowance. Press all seams between block units of odd rows (one, three, five, seven, ...) to the right and all seams between block units of even rows (two, four, six, eight, ...) to the left. When rows are sewn together, seams will butt up against each other and hold each other in place for machine sewing.

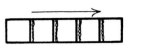
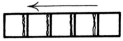

Rows 1, 3, 5, 7...   **Rows 2, 4, 6, 8...**

3. Sew row one to row two, row three to row four, row five to row six, and so on. Sew row unit one-two to row unit three-four and so on. When sewing row *units* together, there will be less bulk than when sewing individual rows together in order. The final row seam will connect the top half of the quilt to the bottom half.

Quilts Set With Sashing

1. Sashing is strips that separate the quilt blocks. Include sashing strips when laying out the quilt to decide on the block arrangement. Sew rows of blocks and vertical sashing strips; press seams toward sashing strips if sashing fabric is darker. Continue sewing blocks to form rows as above.

2. If horizontal sashing strips have no corner setting squares, sew them to block rows. Be careful to align blocks so they match from one row to the next. Press seam allowances toward sashing if sashing fabric is darker.

3. If horizontal sashing strips have corner setting squares, assemble strips and squares for each row. Press the seam allowances *away* from the corner setting squares. These seam allowances will then lay opposite to the seam allowances on the block rows.

4. Row units can be made to reduce bulk as described above in step two of assembling quilts set block to block.

5. When all rows are assembled, add side sashing strips and then end sashing strips.

BORDERS

Stairstep Borders

Note: Check individual quilt directions for sewing order of quilt borders. Crossgrain cuts refers to cuts of fabric made from selvage to selvage.

1. To determine the length of the side borders for any assembled quilt center, measure the length of the quilt from cut edge to cut edge at intervals and take an average of these measurements. *Do not* use the side edge as one of the measurements.

2. Piece crossgrain cuts of fabric to equal the average length of the quilt center or cut seamless borders from fabric on the lengthwise grain. Fold the border and the quilt top into quarters and mark with pins. Matching marker points, pin border to quilt right sides together. If one edge (quilt top or border) is slightly longer, put the longer edge against the feed dog, and the excess fabric will be eased. Take care to see that the pressed seams of the quilt top and border lay flat and do not get twisted.

3. Repeat above process for top and bottom borders.

4. Adding subsequent borders is much easier. The borders previously added can be measured to get the lengths needed for the next ones. Continue adding side borders and then top and bottom borders.

5. Press border seams toward the outside edges of the quilt unless show-through can be prevented by changing pressing directions of border seams.

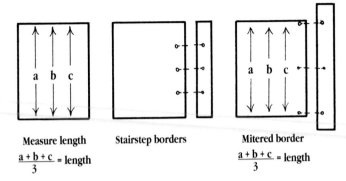

Measure length   **Stairstep borders**   **Mitered border**

$$\frac{a + b + c}{3} = \text{length}$$ $$\frac{a + b + c}{3} = \text{length}$$

Mitered Borders

1. While not difficult, it requires some patience to achieve a terrific mitered corner. To determine the length to prepare the side borders, measure the quilt length without borders as described in step one of stairstep borders above. Add to this measurement the width of all planned borders on both ends of the quilt plus 2″ to 4″ for good measure. (The individual quilt cutting measurements in this book already include this extra fabric.) To determine the length to prepare the end borders, measure the quilt width without borders and add the width of all planned borders on both sides of the quilt plus the 2″ to 4″ extra. Stitch crossgrain cuts of fabric together, if necessary, to make the needed lengths, or cut seamless borders on the lengthwise grain. If the quilt has more than one border, sew individual borders for each side together first to make complete border units. More fabric may be needed, but the corners are much easier to miter. Press seam allowances toward what will be the outside edge of the quilt.

2. Measure the length of the quilt without borders *from seamline to seamline* by measuring down the middle of the quilt in several places, *not* at the edge. Find the center of the long, inside edge of one side border unit and mark it with a pin. From the pin in each direction, measure one-half the quilt length measurement and mark with pins. These marks correspond to the corner seam intersections on the quilt. Find the center of the quilt side by folding and mark it with a pin. Pin side border unit to quilt side right sides together matching corner seam intersections of quilt to corresponding marked points on border; match center. Pin at intervals and stitch; begin and end stitching at corner seam intersections. Repeat for other three borders.

3. Lay a corner of the quilt right side up on an ironing board. The quilt may be pinned to the ironing board to keep it from falling off or being distorted. With borders overlapping, fold one border under to a 45° angle. Match the seams or stripes and work with it until it matches perfectly. The outer edges should be very square and without any extra fullness. Seams and pattern lines should create a 90° angle. Press this fold.

4. Flip outside edge of border with pressed fold over to other outside edge of border right sides together; pin along pressed fold. Stitch from inner corner (about ⅛″ from seamline) to outside of quilt. It may be helpful to baste this seam first. Check the seam for accuracy before stitching.

5. Lay mitered corner of quilt on the ironing board right side up to see if stripes and seams match. Press. Trim mitered seam to ¼″.

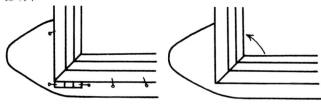

MARKING A QUILT TOP

1. If possible, mark quilting designs on the right side of the quilt top before layering it with backing and batting. It is much easier to work on a hard, flat surface.

2. Quilting designs can be taped to a sunny window. Hold quilt top in position over design and mark lightly with a pencil. Sometimes it is possible to mark quilting designs before the quilt blocks are assembled, which makes marking easier.

3. Many designs can be marked by making a template of the repeated shape. Be sure to make notches on the template where the shapes overlap.

4. If using a stencil, mark lightly and carefully. Connect broken lines by marking freehand.

5. To mark for outline quilting, lay ¼″ masking tape along one side of seam and then quilt next to the other edge of the tape. When finished quilting, simply pick up the strip of tape and reposition it for another quilting line.

PREPARATION OF BACKING AND BATTING
Backing

1. Many quilt tops are wider than one width of fabric. Keep in mind that up to three widths of fabric may be necessary and that joining seams may run vertically *or* horizontally. Figure backing measurements on paper before cutting. Be sure to allow extra width and length.

2. Tear or cut off selvages.

3. Stitch pieces together using a ¼″ seam allowance. Press seams open to eliminate bulk if hand quilting.

Batting

1. If using prepackaged batting, choose the correct size needed, remembering to allow *at least* 2″ or 3″ extra at each side of the quilt.

2. Before using batting, open it out completely a day before it is needed. This allows batting to relax.

3. If using batting sold by the yard, it may be necessary to seam widths together. This is very easily done by butting the batting edges together (not overlapping) and securing them with large, fairly loose whipstitches. Whipstitch on both sides of batting. Take care when quilting not to pull seam apart.

BASTING

1. This step joins the three layers, quilt top, batting, and backing, together in preparation for quilting.

2. Layer the quilt backing (right side down), then the batting, and then the quilt top (right side up). Trim the batting to the same size as the backing.

3. Thread-basting is best for hand quilting projects. Use a long running stitch and catch the three layers every few inches. Start in the center and baste toward the edges in a sunburst design. Roll the backing and batting at the outer edges over to the front; baste in place with large stitches. This will protect the batting. As quilting stitches are added, basting stitches should be removed.

4. Pin-basting can be done with 1″ rustproof safety pins if quilting will be done quickly so they can be removed before they damage the quilt. This method works best for machine quilting. Place pins 4″ to 6″ apart and away from places where quilting lines will be. Edges can be rolled and pinned or left flat.

HAND QUILTING

1. Hand quilting consists of a very tiny running stitch which creates a decorative pattern and holds all three layers of a quilt together. Use a single strand of quilting thread with a tiny knot at one end.

2. Insert the quilting needle through the quilt top and batting but not the backing; bring the needle up where the quilting line will begin. Gently tug the knot so that it slips through the top layer and lodges in the batting.

3. Plant the needle point straight down, lodging the eye end of the needle in one of the thimble indentations, and release the thumb and index finger. To take a stitch, place the thumb on the quilt surface ahead of the needle point and exert a steady pressure on the needle with the thimble finger to push the needle through the fabric. Rock the needle up and down to take several stitches at one time. Make sure the needle is penetrating all layers by placing a finger of the other hand under the quilt where the needle penetrates.

4. To end, make a knot that rests on the quilt top close to the last stitch; insert the needle a stitch length away and run it between the layers for a needle's length. Bring the needle back through the top and tug on the thread to pop the knot into the batting. Cut thread.

5. Outline quilting is quilting done ¼″ from seamlines or applique shapes. It avoids seams and shows up well. "Eyeball" the ¼″, use a pencil line, or quilt next to a piece of ¼″ masking tape. Remove tape when not quilting. Quilting "in the ditch" involves stitching very close to the seamline and is nearly invisible from the top of the quilt. Quilt on the side that does not have the seam allowance. It holds the layers together but does not add another design dimension to the quilt.

MACHINE QUILTING

1. Layer backing, batting, and quilt top as in step two in basting section above. Pin-baste with 1″ rustproof safety pins. Place pins other than where quilting lines will be as they are very difficult to remove while quilting.

2. Use an even-feed foot on the machine. Quilting lines should be placed no more than 4″ apart when using polyester batting. Some options are:
   a. Quilt in the ditch outlining blocks and/or sashing.
   b. Quilt in the ditch between patches every 4″ to 6″.
   c. Quilt straight, parallel lines either diagonally *or* vertically and horizontally by following some of the seams in the patchwork.
   d. Lay ¼″ masking tape down on the quilt top in desired places and stitch next to it.
   e. Mark top lightly with pencil and quilt on pencil line.

3. Use poly/cotton or 100% cotton thread on both the top of the sewing machine and in the bobbin or substitute fine transparent nylon thread for the top thread only. When not using nylon thread, it works best to use the same color thread on the top and in the bobbin.

4. Provide support for the quilt to the left and behind the machine in the form of an extra table. Tightly roll the right side of the quilt to fit through the sewing machine. If quilting parallel lines vertically and horizontally, for example, work on the right half of the quilt first, starting at the edge near the center of the top or bottom border; then flip the quilt around 180° and work on the left half. Repeat for horizontal lines.

5. When sewing, hold the work flat with one hand on each side of the machine foot. Try to open the seam slightly when stitching in the ditch so that when the slight tension is released the stitching "disappears".

TYING

1. Layer backing, batting, and quilt top as in step two of basting section above. Baste using pins or thread.

2. Use perle cotton, six strands of embroidery floss, ⅛″ ribbon, fingering yarn, or fine crochet cotton to tie quilt. A darning needle works well for tying because of its length.

3. Tie quilt at 4″ to 6″ intervals working from the center out.

4. Poke the needle through all layers and come up approximately ⅛″ away. Take an identical stitch directly on top of the first one. Move to the next spot.

5. Repeat step four until thread runs out. Rethread and continue until the whole quilt is caught with these stitches.

6. Clip threads between stitches.

7. Tie a square knot at each point. Trim thread ends.

BINDING

A double binding is recommended because of its durability. Bias strips are not needed unless binding must go around a curved edge.

1. Trim batting and backing even with quilt top.

2. Piece ends of 2½″ wide strips to fit each side of the quilt. Press the binding in half lengthwise wrong sides together.

3. Put binding strips on in the same order the borders were added, usually the side pieces first and then the top and bottom pieces.

4. To apply binding, pin it to the opposite edges of the quilt; pin on the right side and have raw edges even. Stitch using a ⅜″ seam allowance and, if possible, use an even-feed foot to prevent binding from scooting ahead. Bring the binding over the raw edge of the quilt so that the folded edge meets the stitched line on the back. Pin the binding in place on the back of the quilt at each corner.

5. Pin and then stitch the binding to the remaining edges of the quilt as above except allow the binding to extend ½″ at both ends. Turn the extended portion of the binding in before turning it to the back. Handstitch the binding to the back of the quilt at the stitched line.

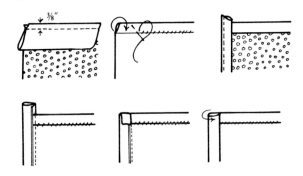

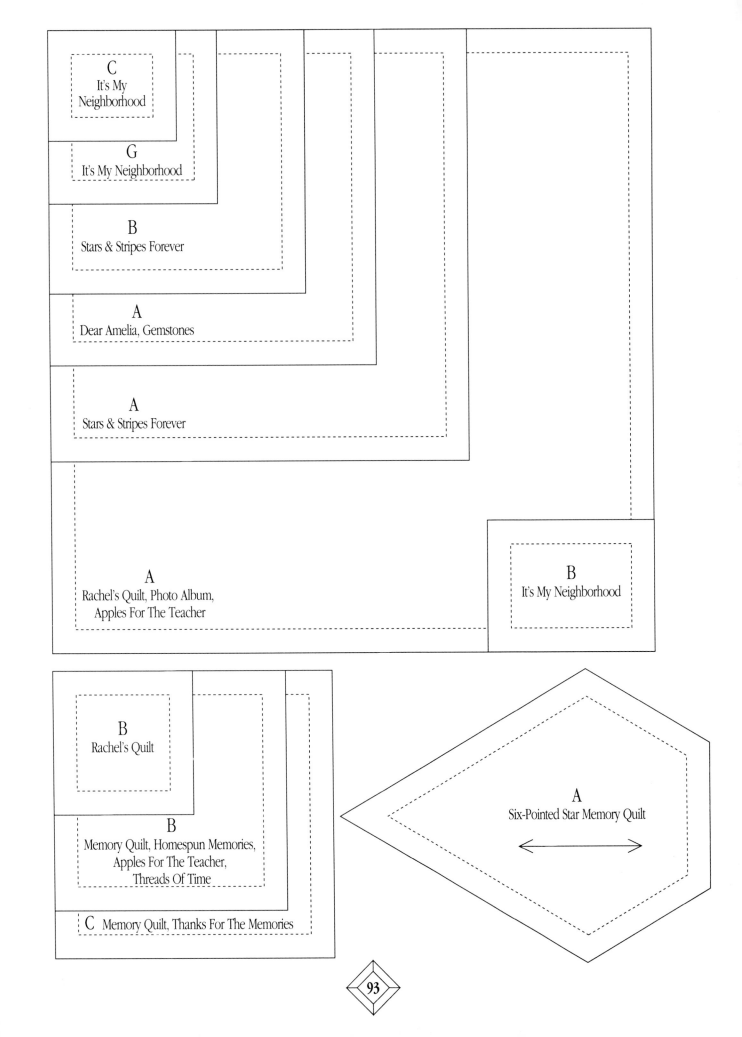

C
It's My
Neighborhood

G
It's My Neighborhood

B
Stars & Stripes Forever

A
Dear Amelia, Gemstones

A
Stars & Stripes Forever

A
Rachel's Quilt, Photo Album,
Apples For The Teacher

B
It's My Neighborhood

B
Rachel's Quilt

B
Memory Quilt, Homespun Memories,
Apples For The Teacher,
Threads Of Time

C   Memory Quilt, Thanks For The Memories

A
Six-Pointed Star Memory Quilt

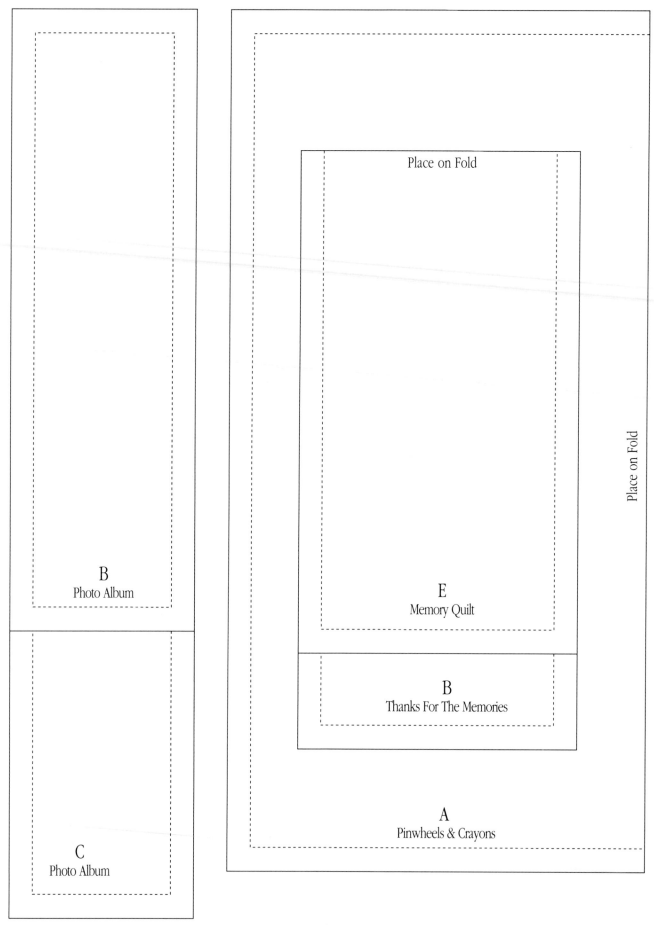

B
Photo Album

C
Photo Album

Place on Fold

E
Memory Quilt

B
Thanks For The Memories

A
Pinwheels & Crayons

Place on Fold

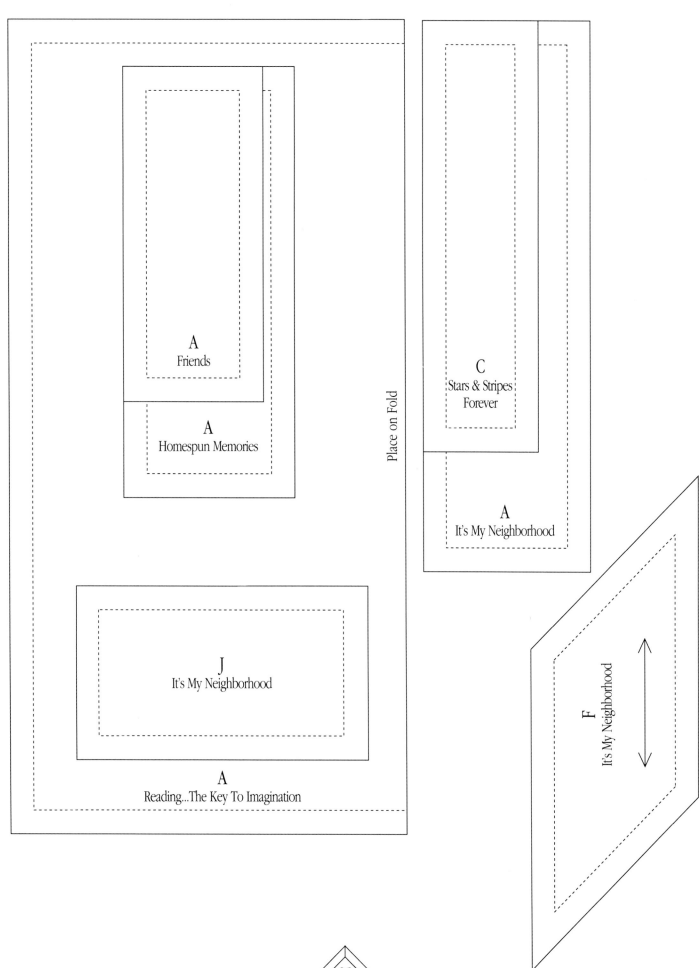

A
Friends

A
Homespun Memories

C
Stars & Stripes
Forever

A
It's My Neighborhood

Place on Fold

J
It's My Neighborhood

A
Reading...The Key To Imagination

F
It's My Neighborhood

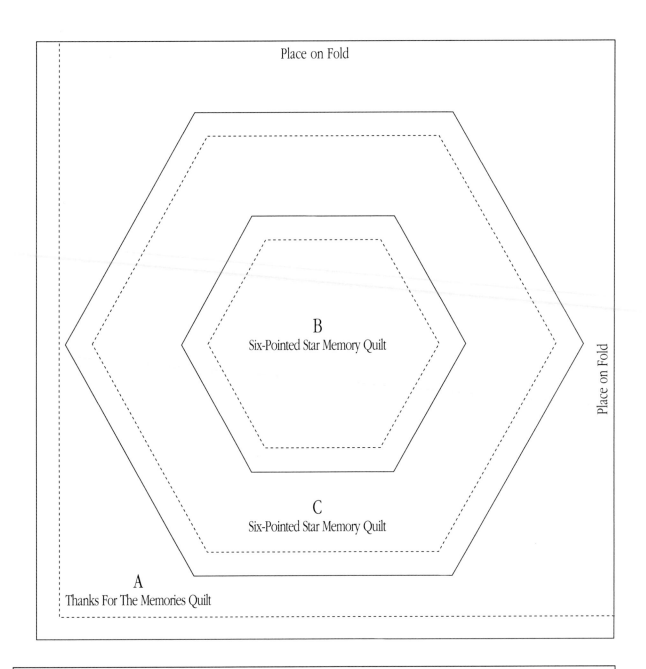

Place on Fold

Place on Fold

B
Six-Pointed Star Memory Quilt

C
Six-Pointed Star Memory Quilt

A
Thanks For The Memories Quilt

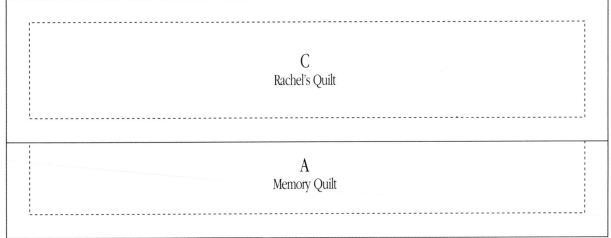

C
Rachel's Quilt

A
Memory Quilt

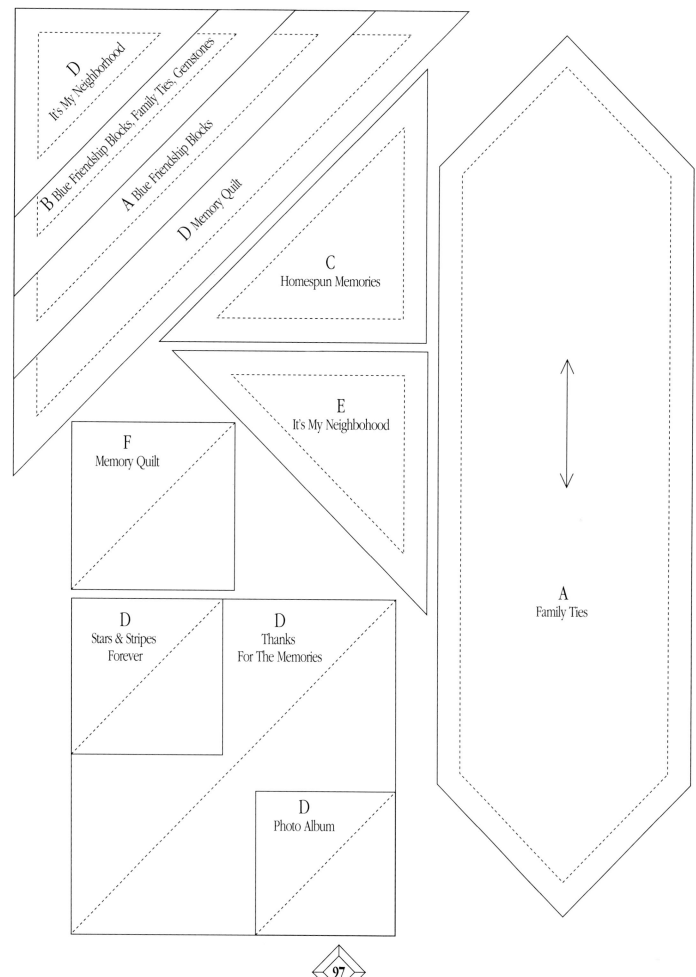

D
It's My Neighborhood

B Blue Friendship Blocks, Family Ties, Gemstones

A Blue Friendship Blocks

D Memory Quilt

C
Homespun Memories

E
It's My Neighbohood

F
Memory Quilt

D
Stars & Stripes
Forever

D
Thanks
For The Memories

D
Photo Album

A
Family Ties

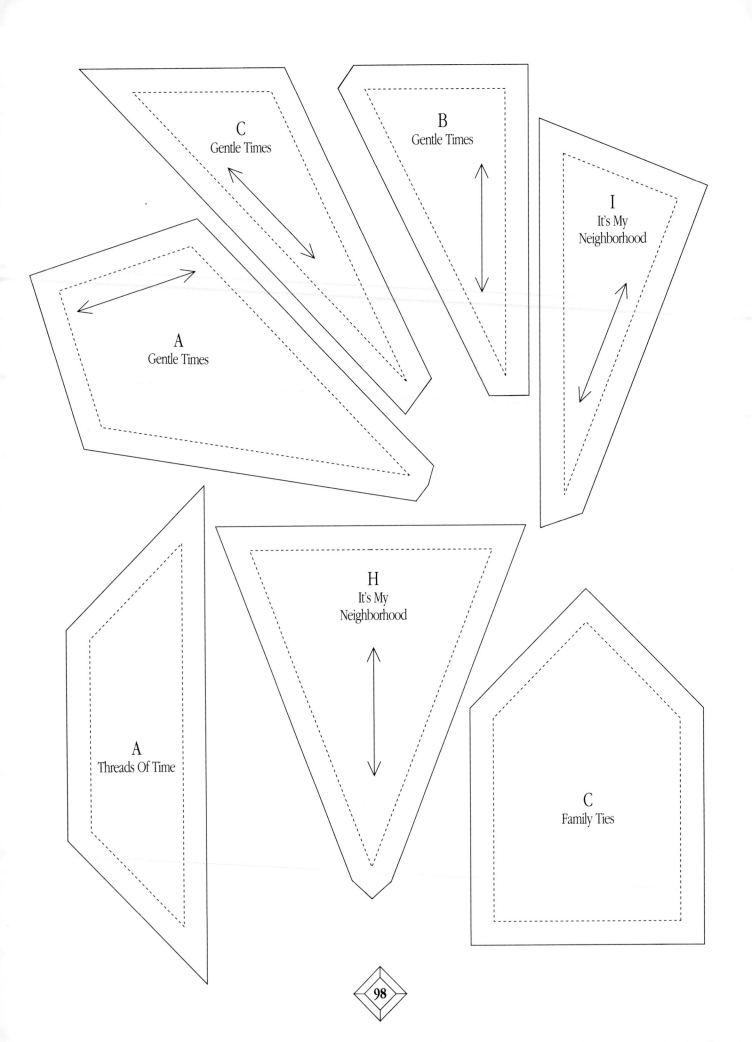

C
Gentle Times

B
Gentle Times

I
It's My
Neighborhood

A
Gentle Times

H
It's My
Neighborhood

A
Threads Of Time

C
Family Ties

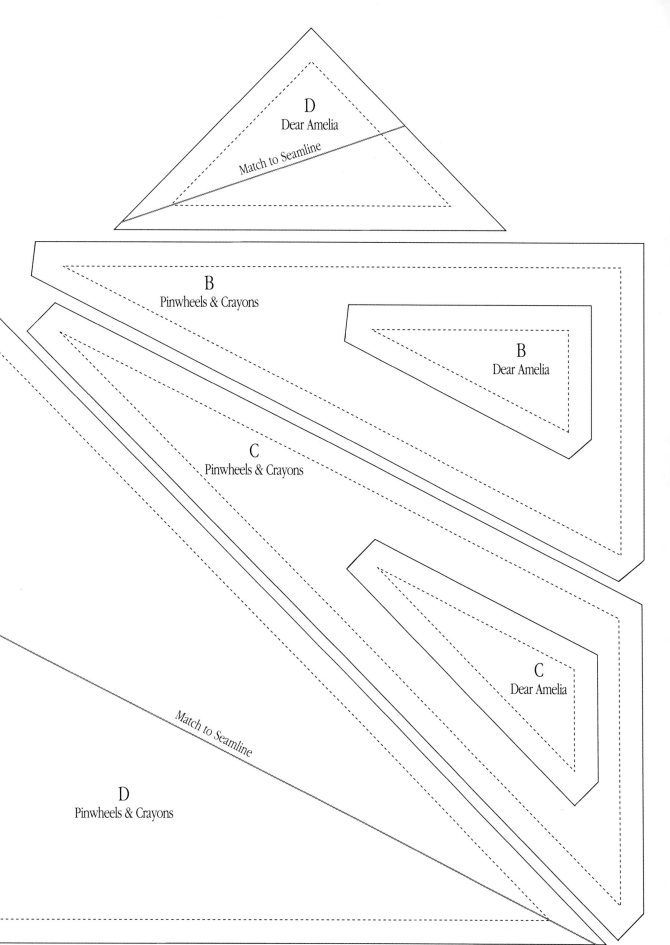

D
Dear Amelia
Match to Seamline

B
Pinwheels & Crayons

B
Dear Amelia

C
Pinwheels & Crayons

C
Dear Amelia

Match to Seamline

D
Pinwheels & Crayons

Quilting Design for Sashing of Memory Quilt

Quilting Design for Gentle Times

Quilting Design for Reading...The Key To Imagination

Quilting Design for Border of Memory Quilt
To fit all three borders, design will need to be
expanded or condensed in length.

Stencils for
School Quilt

See other pattern pages for additional
shapes (hexagon, star, etc.).

BIBLIOGRAPHY

Bond, Dorothy. *Crazy Quilt Stitches.* Dorothy Bond Publisher, 1981.

Croner, Marjorie. *Fabric Photos.* Interweave Press, 1989.

Ferguson, Madonna Auxier. *Creating Memory Quilts.* Betty Boyink Publishing, 1985.

Friendship Quilting. Better Homes and Gardens Books, 1990.

Fry, Gladys-Marie, Ph.D. *Stitched From The Soul: Slave Quilts from the Ante-Bellum South.* Dutton Studio Books, 1990.

Hall, Carolyn Vosburg. *Friendship Quilts By Hand And Machine.* Chilton Book Company, 1988.

Hargrave, Harriet. *Heirloom Machine Quilting.* C & T Publishing, 1990.

Houck, Carter. *The Quilt Encyclopedia Illustrated.* Harry N. Abrams, Inc., Publishers, 1991.

Kolter, Jane Bentley. *Forget Me Not.* Sterling Publishing Company, Inc., 1990.

Lipsett, Linda Otto. *Remember Me: Women and Their Friendship Quilts.* The Quilt Digest Press, 1985.

Malone, Maggie. *1,001 Patchwork Designs.* Sterling Publishing Company, Inc., 1982.

McKelvey, Susan. *Friendship's Offering.* C & T Publishing, 1990.

Miles, Elaine. *Many Hands: Making a Communal Quilt.* Delta Lithograph Company, 1982.

Nadelstern, Paula and LynNell Hancock. *Quilting Together: How to Organize, Design, and Make Group Quilts.* Crown Publishers, Inc., 1988.

Ohrbach, Barbara Milo. *A Token of Friendship.* Clarkson N. Potter, Inc., 1987.

Ruskin, Cindy. *The Quilt: Stories From The NAMES Project.* Pocket Books, 1988.

Shirer, Marie. *Quilt Settings.* Moon Over The Mountain Publishing Company, 1989.

Shirer, Marie. *The Quilter's How-To Dictionary.* Leman Publications, Inc., 1991.

Smith, Lois Tornquist. *Fun and Fancy Machine Quiltmaking.* American Quilter's Society, 1989.

Wells, Jean and Marina Anderson. *A Celebration of Hearts.* C & T Publishing, 1988.